T0029742

"In From the Lost and Found Department we encounter a poet's vast witness of and homage to the world. In the aftermath of unspeakable violence and cruelty, Joy Kogawa pulls us aside and says, Look here, what matters are the small fish, the mundane kindnesses, the love that remains despite catastrophes. Kogawa is a writer who has powerfully impacted Canadian discourses, and her latest book is a necessary addition to any reader's collection."

—Tsering Yangzom Lama, author of
We Measure the Earth with Our Bodies

"Each poem in Joy Kogawa's From the Lost and Found Department permeates into the crevices of the everyday and travels towards silvery seams of wisdom and the denials of history. They pierce with humour and delicacy. No topic is too small or too large for Kogawa's audacious attention. In this volume is the enduring work of a committed life, where every surface is turned and transformed."

—Phoebe Wang, author of Waking Occupations

"Through the forests of history, the fog of memory, the floating faith of a dream, Joy Kogawa's poems seek—and achieve—deep clarity and grace. Whether recollecting wartime dispossession and displacement, travels through Japan, or the loss of loved ones, Kogawa's lucid lines evince tender, sensuous attention to the 'cracks in the curtains / of the universe,' those moments when the ephemeral and the eternal converge. From the Lost and Found Department asks us to hear 'the sound / of hands / clapping like lightning,' to hold 'a deep purple kimono bought / in some vaguely remembered girlhood,' and to acknowledge that 'it's our duty' to 'greet the dead who smile through trees . . .'"

—Michael Prior, author of Burning Province

FROM
THE LOST
AND FOUND
DEPARTMENT

Books by Joy Kogawa

POETRY

The Splintered Moon (1967)

A Choice of Dreams (1974)

Jericho Road (1977)

Six Poems (1980)

Woman in the Woods (1985)

A Song of Lilith (2000)

A Garden of Anchors: Selected Poems (2003)

What Do I Remember of the Evacuation?
(Illustrated by Tyler Jenkins) (2009)

NOVELS

Obasan (1981)

Itsuka (1992) (Published as Emily Kato in 2005)

The Rain Ascends (1995, 2003)

NONFICTION

Gently to Nagasaki (2016)

East of the Rockies (2019)

CHILDREN'S LITERATURE

Naomi's Road (Illustrated by Matt Gould) (1986, 2005)

Naomi's Tree (Illustrated by Ruth Ohi) (2009)

FROM
THE LOST
AND FOUND
DEPARTMENT

New and Selected Poems

JOY KOGAWA

McClelland & Stewart

Copyright © 2023 by Joy Kogawa
Introduction copyright © 2023 by Brandon Shimoda

This edition published 2023

McClelland & Stewart and colophon are registered trademarks of
Penguin Random House Canada Limited.

Published simultaneously in the United States of America by McClelland & Stewart, a division
of Penguin Random House Canada Limited.

Library and Archives Canada Cataloguing in Publication data is available upon request.

ISBN: 978-0-7710-0513-8
ebook ISBN: 978-0-7710-0514-5

The Splintered Moon: copyright © 1967 Joy Kogawa, first published by Fiddlehead Poetry Books
in 1967; A Choice of Dreams: copyright © Joy Kogawa, first published by McClelland & Stewart
in 1974; Jericho Road: copyright © Joy Kogawa, first published by McClelland & Stewart in 1977;
Woman in the Woods copyright © Joy Kogawa, first published by Mosaic Press in 1985; A Garden
of Anchors: Selected Poems copyright © Joy Kogawa first published by Mosaic Press in 2003.

Cover design by Talia Abramson
Cover art: Jeff Goode / Toronto Star / Getty Images
Typeset in Seria by M&S, Toronto
Printed in Canada

McClelland & Stewart,
a division of Penguin Random House Canada Limited,
a Penguin Random House Company
www.penguinrandomhouse.ca

1 2 3 4 5   27 26 25 24 23

Penguin
Random House
McCLELLAND & STEWART

For my parents

Contents

The Splintered Moon

A Choice of Dreams

About Japan

Down Through Generations: an introduction
to Joy Kogawa's *From the Lost and Found
Department: New and Selected Poems*

by Brandon Shimoda

> the love
> is the root
> is the root of the dark
> Joy Kogawa, hey jude

I woke one morning to someone telling me that there is a new book
of poetry by Joy Kogawa and that it is called From the Lost and Found
Department. A ball of light bounded across the sky, through the window,
into my room. I was returned, in that moment, to my first encounter
with Joy Kogawa. Except I have no memory of it. The experience is so
fresh it has not passed into memory. And yet it was a long time ago.
When I do not remember the first time, I replace the unformed memory
with the understanding that there was no first, but always. I was returned
to always (itsuka). I wondered, is the Lost and Found Department where
Joy Kogawa is from? Is it comprised of what she recovered there? A
department formed around a giving, gravitational field?—What was
lost? Was it stolen, forgotten? Found by grace or does one have to sift?
Through time, names, a debris of words.—Am I assuming the poet into
this, instead of a presence of which she is a part? The ball of light, like
hinotama: the revelation, the undivided attention, of the soul. From the
Lost and Found Department has come to rest in the everyday.

I do remember, however, my first encounter with Joy Kogawa's poetry.
It followed my relationship with a book that has, for me, always existed:
Obasan. But the poetry came first, as the opening of Obasan intimates:
There is a silence that cannot speak. There is a poem in Joy Kogawa's first
full-length collection, A Choice of Dreams (1974)—a book especially
meaningful to me—in which a westerner is searching, ludicrously, for

something to eat in Ginza, Tokyo ("Lost Man at the Tourist Information Centre"). He makes his way through a sea of *strange bobbing creatures* to the beacon of a Lost and Found booth. Good joke, because that is where you go when you are looking for something you lost, not if you are lost or looking for yourself. A woman is behind the counter. She blinks at the westerner, flips through a directory, sends the westerner away. At this point, Joy Kogawa—in the composition; she too is hungry and looking—transforms the westerner, even more lost now, into a barnyard animal, bewildered and bellowing in a cityscape of *abstract choreography.* The poem, cubist-surrealist, is wild yet unassuming. It is tucked into a series of poems in which Joy Kogawa recorded the experience of her first visit to Japan, 1969. She, second-generation Japanese Canadian, was returning to a place she had never been, each moment, each encounter, disordering and redefining the sense of what it means to return to a place one has never been. I apprehend in these poems and in Joy Kogawa's poetry, the cultivation of consciousness as synonymous with the clarification—and the liberation—of identity as the act of paying insurgent, uncanny attention not only to what you are looking for, but through. The cultivation is ongoing, if you let it be, is life.

As I think of the poems that unfold for me a map of how to be a Nikkei westerner, a yonsei poet, of how to look long to the high hillside grave of ancestors and at what is growing at breath's-length, I see Joy Kogawa, radiant with expectancy, waiting her turn to root meticulously through a collection of suspended debris, to recognize, hopefully and miraculously, her own.

It is as though Joy Kogawa left the Lost and Found booth in Ginza, and was transported, by translucent wormhole, carrying all of herself, down through generations, into the present day. Just in time. From the Lost and Found Department, where cherry blossoms are falling, leaves are dancing, disintegrating, fruit is plunging earthward. There are three worms. Two veins. Many people, named (artist Aiko Suzuki died in 2005, poet/artist Roy Kiyooka died in 1994, Barry Kermit Gostlin, Mike, Jack and Olivia, Metta, Russell, Ted, Yoshiko, Gordon...) and unnamed, every portrait the drawing of a process. Not still life, still living.

In time, every portrait becomes an elegy. To the one written. To the one, through the love they feel for others, writing.—What you look at, you become. What looks at you becomes you.—It comes all at once, unhurriedly. The first intake of breath, which joins, on the circle of life, the last. The lure, the root, in this we trust; dust we go, dust and dream, in the light of this new dreaming; morning's light, sunlight, rainlight, twilight; we'll crash into it, catch it, drink it, ladders of it; the light follows follows follows follows, burns out; no time for dying. Joy Kogawa's poetry, generous of heart, is able to do everything that poetry, as a condition, a refraction, a reorientation, can do. From the Lost and Found Department is comprised of supplications, benedictions, acts of defiance, of reliance, kinematics, cosmologies reflected in momentary floods evaporating, entire retrospectives in a poem, a line, kakekotoba, kireji, haboku, hokku-like thresholds facing out and into the world. Compassion, suffering with. Mercy, grace. Gratitude. Abundance, giving completely.

Returning to always (itsuka). Joy Kogawa was the first writer of Japanese descent, born and who lived outside of Japan, who I read, who I had heard of. She was certainly the first I read who wrote about the incarceration of people of Japanese ancestry in North America, WWII, even more certainly in the ways she has. She was six when her family was exiled to Slocan, British Columbia, before being resettled in Coaldale, Alberta. It was her experience, and the lifelong reaching back to retrieve it from being, by force and forgetting, erased, that introduced me to incarceration, not the experiences of my own family members, who were incarcerated in the United States (Fort Missoula, Heart Mountain, Poston), about which I, mournfully yet mundanely, knew nothing. It was a displaced revelation, another country first, literature being that too.

The glorious, coruscating, necessarily frustrated overture of Obasan became my mission statement: If I could follow the stream down and down to the hidden voice, would I come at last to the freeing word? I took the question, and the lack of a reply, into my relationship with the past, embodied by my grandfather. I put my body into my ear, slipped into the stream. It was the beginning, for me, of poetry. I used to think, before then, that to commune with my ancestors, I had to wait for them to come down. That they formed a pantheon somewhere above, beyond the upper limit of imagination. That they descended, like dancers on long, ethereal silks. But maybe, according to how Joy Kogawa's question, and to how, in its realization, poems are made, how they make me feel and how my mind falls with them, to be a descendant means more simply to be the one who descends. That the ancestors are not above, but below, where roots listen intently.

Fundamental to awareness is loss, to intimacy, loss. Something occurs to me while reading From the Lost and Found Department: that when you spend your life, or a good portion of it, looking—reaching—for someone or something that is out of reach, you find yourself in deeper relation with who and what is around you. In beholding, embracing, absence, you become attuned—to everything. The peripheries are centered, everything stands on end. The abstract choreography is transfigured into a reception that brushes against you like homecoming. Now you are humble, disarmed. Open. To what is here, before you.

One night, sleeping in a temple in Japan, Joy Kogawa was visited by two words: mercy and abundance. She wrote them down, fell back to sleep. I envy you who have never read anything by Joy Kogawa. I envy you who have read one thing, many things. I envy you who have read everything. Most of all I envy the poems, for achieving a sentience that is salutation, being present for the arrival not of oneself, but of others, and to inaugurate, lovingly, the space of their experience:

goodbye goodbye, Joy Kogawa writes.
we never said goodbye, she writes.
hello hello, she is writing.

Brandon Shimoda is the author of several books of poetry and prose, including The Grave on the Wall, which received the PEN Open Book Award, and Hydra Medusa.

FROM
THE LOST
AND FOUND
DEPARTMENT

From the Lost and
Found Department

2023

AS APOLOGY DOES

among trinkets in a box
of sorrowing beads
necklaces, scarves, umbrellas
hats, gloves, socks
watches in the
lost and found department

names drifting in a
stream of words a
debris of words during
a recent shower during
a small momentary flood

in this indelicate place
the word integrity
one so delicate friend wore
on his lapel or in
his heart how
is one ever to know

except that integrity is
lost neither by
deluge nor judgment

come let us walk together
on the emmaus road

companionship
of sad news

as the petals fall
as the seed grows

at the end of our journey
we glimpse a stranger

hand holding the
bread as it is blest

we'll see the light
and how it follows

follows follows follows
wherever the bread goes

he is crouching
in a corner of a bombed garden
cultivating a single green hair
half a fingernail high
when her letter arrives
and his body fills with earth
hard brown seeds
break open pushing
fine green fur
through tiny pores

he becomes a lawn
for her walking
undulant with oxygen
but as he reads
winged lizards
leap from the page
tiny dragons
breathe fire over
the unsuspecting countryside

her letter bombs
her fire words
and his charred yard
a minefield
of metal words
and a sculpture of air
crouching there

i think at age now seventy-four
as one more lately born
though i be short-lived ant or flower
or enduring stone i might
receive less scorn

dear friend-child my
torn with which falsehood
shall i reach you
who through hell's torment
have prevailed

this lie then, this:
the blood in which we flail
the currency of theft, of
molten gold, is
thicker far than all

never should we say
never did we love
for there was one
midweek day
and a long waiting
into disappearance
until met
and met
and met
in rockcliffe
in sunlight
and our day arrived
sap full flowing

no, love
was not a mistake
love is an explosion
that flies through dwarf stars
and is not extinguished

ON MEMORY LOSS

let's not rush to retirement homes
while leaves and autumn still leave
in late november our limbs
less limber less spritely though
not yet brittle not yet

BLACKFLY

in the buzz
of the aged brain
atrophied

a blackfly
bats against a
window

from the edge
of the web
a spider

late autumn
she grows
fat

I THRUST YOU AWAY

because, one could say
the fall into
Zorba the Greek or
infancy, a hand
snapping a twig
or a thumb on the
pulse in the neck
just where a
knife might cut
and a trickle
of volcanic blood
because the magma i
thrust you away
because breath demands
breath and the gasp
fell out of my lungs fled
down my arm because
kite strings because
silver umbilical cords the
clamp the tourniquet

I DID NOT SEE

yesterday's blood moon
nor do i see
your mother weeping
in the morning
I hear you whispering
and my beloved
a millstone
for the unforgivable
round his neck
under the water
sinking
sinking
with forgiveness

BORROWING KNEES
  for Barry Kermit Gostlin

unsprung
your big day
drifts through
the april forever party
in times parallel

you who are
and were not
i lend you my knees
in the unbidden
incense of applause
that rises from the bog
of that last day

dust to infantile
dust we go
stalking the spaces
the moment's
window and
—hush—
rag doll there
limbless now and
purpling

look, barry, look
when we kneel
we can see
the sound
of hands
clapping like lightning

FOR A GATEKEEPER

she suffered from your act
o gatekeeper

moon and memory
mix at the altar

her ongoing sighs
penetrate the night

you who stand guard
grotesque with authority

held her heaven
at bay

in my grief
i hold her torment

that you kissed her
on her lips

and she was gripped
forever

MOONLIGHT

luminous
as moonlight
is the glow
of the sun's
reflection

he sits
among the halt
the lame
the blind

clink

a metallic morsel
into an outstretched
paper cup

IN MARPOLE

full throated
white cherry blossoming
in the lane

mama's pure
soprano

in the land of mercy
in the land of
the second chance

IN THE VALLEY OF THE BLIND

no one can look
at the sun without filters

in the valley of the blind
the sighted must submit

HOW DO I THANK THEE

let me thank the excitement of
the orchestra warming up

the bubbles that bounce up
in mid-sentence

the mysteries of fingertips undiscovered
undisclosed and overly attended by caution

for these the demons in their moments scoff
for demons I thank thee not

yet too soon they will depart as will
all flesh but while at bay

I extend voluminous thanks
from these so sharkless shores

BUREAUCRATS

bureaucrats may kill
more people than they save

eichmann
kept his job

the elevator waits
for the push of a button

receive them
as sunlight, rainlight
intended smiles
in passing
not smirks
not scorn
not mockery
so received perhaps
by a windblown soil

small breaths
as an infant
born still,
and grey
until that first
intake
the first
cry
the first
struggle
and the joy
that attends

STEWED CHERRY

eating the stewed
cherry this morning
the stem still clinging
to the fruit
the fruit still
clinging and remembering
the child the plane crash
her hand still clutching
the disembodied arm
of her mother

as surely as leaves of cherry tree
lean towards moon
so surely do tendrils of my heart lean
however dense the dark
however deep the fissures of harm
by habit and intent I trust
the footsteps of the voice
that named my name

PORTRAIT OF THE ARTIST AS DONKEY
for Aiko Suzuki

we waken, both of us
she who is god knows where
i rush along in the subway
she doggedly energetic
my fellow donkey friend
touched by the sun
struck with determination
in the mad sunrise of our
ancient gam-ba-re heritage
two wild women toiling
for the earth spirit festival

she lives as much as do I
along the squealing subway wheels
the strobe lights of windows flashing
past flashing past

excesses of farewells her arms signalling
semaphores

see it
believe it
the poster declares and
i do

all the way up subway stairs
to street level toronto twilight
the sky glowing rapturous pink
to grey reflecting in windows

we belong to legions of donkeys
aiko and I subterranean donkeys
labouring for all we're worth into our
sunsets

dear point nine
dragon slayer how
could I not believe
at an advanced age
daily miracles
the tiny new leaf
in my dormant orchid
hailing bright greenly
and whether to flower
or no alive
alive oh

HELLO GRASS

in toronto flat pave
ment and con
crete land hello
martyr trees dis
connected

all life is grass, caesar
and non-life is full
metal life-size cows
here in perfect
milklessness

but hello hello
wet green
blade

because he loves the cello
its bow low over
the abdomen of the soul
thick and swarming
with all that is sordid
and soaring and therefore
although he is in flight
from the weeping
in the streets of the city
still I trust him because
he loves the cello

because somewhere in
the morning's light
the cellist weeps
in the streets of the city
dissolving walls
with her bow's deep
utterances and he
who loves the cello
will pause

bach; magician
his brandenburg concertos
making the thinly clad lady
the crown placed on her
unlikely head she basks
in applause till at last she
steps off stage to the back door
back from bach to the
back alley where she lives
raking the cinders underfoot
and humbled by elbow-driven
self-involved pigeons

dear prince or coachman
it is long past midnight
and the pitiable world
scurries underfoot
but wasn't she gorgeous tonight
the harpsichord i mean

meanwhile she is standing
in the shadows
watching the prince who
holds the glass slipper of
a princess he does not recognize

MAY 18, 2022
    for Miso

today she departs
your furry purry companion
in a time of lilac and lavender
pad padding along
through the soft undergrowth
in the jungle of your daze

on the unending trail
of gently scattered petals
miso mews as she goes

may 18, 2022
we loved each other well
my human danielle
goodbye goodbye

the love
is the root
is the root of the dark

thirty pieces of silver
your price and you are
welcome to it

on the sour hillside
bones destined
find cold comfort in cold cash

you will never have enough
the hate
will not abate

here in a back alley on
sacred ground a wounded tree
weeps for her child

slain in a churchyard
in north vancouver
furtively surreptitiously

MOZART AND ROBIN

for Senator Nancy Ruth

watching cyclists
rippling along the gardiner
sunday morning

and wondering about
silenced robin
that its full story resides

within the same waters
in which mozart continues
to swim upstream

early grey october days
5:00 a.m. up scott across berczy
through the park at st. james
and back down following
red parade profuse in mid-air
mike's bouquets his
antidote to urban blight in this
corner of the universe he loved
beauty becomes us, he says
beauty
becomes
us

THE QUEEN

takes in her arms
the poorest man she knows
who spends his time in a counting house
counting out his pennies

in the parlour while
eating bread eating eating bread
she dreams her honey
will come to her soon

the maid has stopped
hanging clothes and has fled with a flock
of royal purple bluebirds
robed in sunlight

MIGRATING BIRDS

three black and white tiny birds
dead
on the sidewalk

a mad woman
holds them out
to black and white strangers

thin high conversations
crash into the light

NOTICE

notice the beanstalk growing
through the fontanelle
of the baby as she scans
her mother's eyes
fixed on her phone
notice the voracious hunger
in the baby climbing climbing
for all she's worth up and up
and the beanstalk starting to
collapse

ON STONES

pick up stones
aim at head
or heart or anywhere
on the kneeling body

tasukete kudasai, dad said
please help

the only way i can help
is to stand with him
stand with him
stand with him
until i am brought to my knees

here on my knees
the molotov cocktail
torch gasoline target flaming match
and every bitter berry she's gathered

A PARENT'S LOVE IS DEEP

my father said
oya no ai wa fukai
as his son
derided and
abandoned him
privately publicly
whom once
he had adored

whatever horrors
my oya did
our triumph is
derision's
not forever

PUMICE

molten rock
down mountainside
to water

lava
porous
floating stone

how beautiful on the mountains
the feet of those who bring
good news

EXPLANATION

because the flying insects are
attracted to the light
the spider on the
outside of the window
spins spins spins
grows fat

FOR DEIDRE JAN

my little girl sweet singing
four-year-old, hands clasped, pudgy baby i
long for her though now fully fledged
mother barn swallow still singing
through foraging skies sleek and sinewy
and bringing nourishment to her straw nest
her wide open-beaked babies my doting
mother/child with as much attentiveness
as this world affords, my one my only
daughter when is daughter's day

orange memories of
orange scarves orange t-shirts, orange-speckled
dresses orange roses on the steps of the new
city hall in lethbridge
this august 26 2011 friday
twilight candles more visible
as orange moves to dark
dear jack how the light in which
you swim ignites this
country from town to town singing
early one morning just as
the sun is rising
i hear a country pleading
in voices sad and low
oh don't you grieve us oh
never leave us—

CHRISTMAS 2019
   for Metta

three-toed pigeon tracks
a strutting bird once
upon a not yet set
sidewalk and what
footprints will we leave, you and I
as we too strut on this
speck of dust and dream

we have criss-crossed our sidewalks
scratch by blotch by lofty intent
while the snows fall the winds howl vertical
and the world blows flat as toast

meanwhile rung by rung
up ladders of light
we hop we flop we wing our way
and always
that which we call Love
always and always

FOR ROY KIYOOKA

we never said goodbye
roy but you sudden as disappearance
were the way of the maze full of energy

roy as birdcry and windsong roy as
audacity dancing as goodbye

mistress muse mistress music
gather your alphabet singer
meticulous shaper and scraper
of wordbones your scaler of timewalls
your seer your painter of pear trees
and shadows

here in this january mourning wave our
last telephone small words *okay seeya*
and click the tiny amen taking it for granted

hansel my brother
we are babes
in the lost woods of
many paths many
coloured stones leading
us home we are not
led to a gingerbread
devouring but home
where we rest inviolate
beneath the trees the
autumn leaves dancing
dancing like ours
in our rusting hair

FOR TED

on the floor in a huddle around a candle
ted dianne and me and mary lou sometimes
wednesday after 7 to 9 p.m. wednesday

pacing the hallways of our hearts
we wade through the waters we
enter the deep beyond our mundane lives
practising peace practising presence and
sometimes imagining the final run through
the tunnel of the shadow

our conversation from the heights
is not by death ended and with
our open circle of witnesses
elliot andre leonard dave patricia
joan floyd rebecca
we seed the skies
with words without words

gladly boldly needfully
we drink the light
and are captured by light
and in the light of this new dreaming
ted's hearty hallelujah his loud amen
whispers here among us
ted in our circle still standing beside
beautiful elaine
our kind beloved elaine

FOR YOSHIKO

we will always know
she was the best
we would ask

what would yoshiko
say now? what
would she do?

our morning star
she of the kindest eyes

FRIDGE DOOR CLOSING

metallic cold of fridge door thud
my father I have carried you carried you carried you
alone in the wilderness of bewilderment
where lurks your unacceptable your reptilian lust

i will not deny my love for you nor hide it
nor flee to safety

now arrives endless rage now that you are safely dead
thank God
your tormented and tormenting life is done
and as surely as overripe fruit plunges earthward
so too does hatred come my way

in the freezing dark
outside the fridge door snowflakes
sweet chariots coming
for to carry me home

gathering eyes in the garden
while the house is burning down

the fashion industry

BUTTERFLY

the monarch
on her ornate august wings
crossing city street
brick wall and up, up, up,
to roof and relentlessly
onward frail butterfly
downwind again
fluttering descent
along treetops and
out of sight
out of blue
autumn applause
toronto auditorium

CHESHIRE CAT

this morning the moon
is a cheshire cat
disappearing
with its thin smile
into the orange dawn
into the bright
black purple clouds

the fumble of
a plane heads for
home a speck of an island
in lake ontario

home where
our thin smiles live
before disappearing

CHILD MODEL

help me someone, she said softly
undramatically
posing on a small curved bridge
over the goldfish pond

help me someone, she said
squinting into the camera's
blinking eye

she dangled her tiny feet
over the edge and slid into
the shallow pool
where bright goldfish
swam for display

CHRISES

sleeping crumpled bag
in urine-soaked city
stairwell concrete corner
and black word
scrawled large
on streaky wall

chrises

christ of poverty
we are in crisis

every night you
rest in pieces
rags and rages
and contra
dictions

CLIFF-LEAPING

as prelude to flight
or cliff-leaping as
first lesson in flying
every moment
a readiness
by cliff hanger
cliff hugger
non-flying wingless pebble
leaper of little falling
wedded to rock and
untransposed to air
to cliff hunger

COINCIDENTS

cracks in the curtains
of the universe—these
quirks
laugh bites
snacks
surprise us
between meals

CONSTELLATION

night of navigation
on turbulent seas
stars direct

three philpotts
elmore stuart lisa
align with north star

HE ASPIRED TO POLITICS
for Anton

an old campaign button
among many others
in my bathroom

a helicopter
disappearing in
a cloudy january sky

thursday morning
thirty-third floor
exercise room

an unusually warm
winter day but
winter nonetheless

and disintegrated leaves
beneath the
disappeared snow

FOOTNOTE AND TITLE

he offered me
a footnote
in his book

i offered him
title
to mine

we both swam away
in swift currents

late toronto morning
august 24 2011
gasping to nathan phillips square
before rain washes tributes in chalk
to jack layton

almost there almost
past adelaide up bay to queen
as downpour
and multicoloured chalk
sluices down ramp
pink and yellow words

and in the rain
one old man with no
umbrella and no
hair and right hand
trembling

WALKING WITH STUART

along the humber
water over stone

somalia armenia
a cemetery
brown and black caterpillar
charming and courteous garden
beneath eglinton avenue bridge

many dandelions with
heads as white as ours
in the shady woods
on the first gentle
day of june

AIDE FAMILY SUNDAY

at the church of the holy
trinity "make the puzzle
complete" i said to bill who
said "there's a poem
there" as we laughed
and passed
his peace intact
my piece not yet
in its location
somewhere perhaps in
the blueness of the
sky or water who
can tell with blues and
our many busy peaces

REMEMBERING MAMA

walking through the eaton centre
in toronto and remembering
mama buying the green dress
when we drove through cranbook
how she'd loved fashion

and her wide-brimmed white hat
she'd bought before the war
in vancouver how it became
old and yellow in coaldale
how jauntily she wore it
the hat pin securing the bun

ordinary moments before
the mighty typhoon
swept happiness away forever
how we became trees
to be cut down forever
and all the walking past forever
and mama silent henceforth forever

DENIAL

snowflake
proudly unique
denies the ocean

cherry blossom
falling delicately
denies nanking

WORD STONES

walking through woods
with careful words
pocketed
in tight fists
not dropped not
marking a pathway

my stone words
dear one
untimely and
whispering
into the wind

at midnight
how I love you
and how you
will never know

you make drumsticks
you make a poem of wood
you leap in the air you rush
towards a door intending
to knock knock knock you see
it beginning to open from
the other side and a
shaft of light on a
green shoot meanwhile
underground with
roots listen intently

MAY SHE WHO IS PERFECT

feel the heft of claims, its target
thud on left arm near shoulder the
second directly beneath the
navel a third and fourth on
buttocks as she turns to protect
her head which nevertheless
receives a sharp edge on the crown
where the comb had carefully
divided the part and hey the
head is dented the lungs
fail and gasp into the night

A WRINKLE APPEARED

in the path of the moon
a spontaneous laugh
a vein being pruned

KAGAN'S FLOWERS

pink, yellow, more pink
mom's water jug
delicate, time touched

time's thread is a tale
the heart trusts even
through the scissoring

still life beckons
time's ever lasting
ample arms

LOVE IS A FIRE

and i am a thin
green branch
wishing to be consumed
if i could love
i would be so busily burning
that when the light
is finally out
i would have had
no time
for dying

FOR GORDON AT SEVEN

what an extremist you were
nebuchadnezzar
always threatening to
kill off people by
sword by fire and
limb from limb

in this suburb lives
a small Daniel daring and
daring to worship no
gods of mine and heaven
help him he saunters off
among wild beasts in
dungeons of my creating
yet daily he is back safely
oh praise the god of small
extremist here whose
name may be daniel or
nebuchadnezzar i
don't really know who he is
or who i am in relation to him
but somehow we are both here
every day testing testing
1, 2, 3, 4, testing are you
there god?

DANIEL

sound of horn, pipe, lyre,
trigon, harp, bagpipe
and every kind of music
in fiery furnace
where no flame destroys
fire-dancers
fire-eaters
fire-singer fire-walker

MIDNIGHT WALK

mama taking her two young children
late at night snowstorm
me wadded with woollens
past backyard past streetlight
past house of english missionary
snow mounds on fence posts
silence piling up the air too cold
daddy at home preparing penitential meal
how too unusual how too strange
what wrong had he done

christmas morning storybooks baby kittens
it couldn't be undone

DUAL CITIZENSHIP

the sorcerer king remains
between wake and sleep
wielding his forgetfulness sword

he has covered the path
with leaves
which on waking we sweep

in our efforts to retain
dual citizenship
the thin road as it
crosses to day

AT THE GATES
for Russell

the casket
the friends
the tears i
the photographs
should not
the chatter
have come
next time how
better go the
boats down to
how better the sea
for whose sake
am i not mine
here not his

SPLIT-LEVEL HOUSE

for not being the smiling
cookie-baking stepford mother in
our split-level suburban house

for staring at the black and white
square kitchen tiles proceeding
diagonally then otherwise

my darling children
for the hours I spent sleepwalking
in the clean house clean

the rest of the family loved

dancing on tilting deck
clutching the promise
the lure
the root
in this we trust
in dust
our salvific
calf

when holding your last tooth you said
"I must say thank you tooth
serving my long life"

you were a painful tooth, dad
you fled to the other side of the moon
where there is weeping and gnashing

mama lost her teeth to pregnancy
she bequeathed her love of truth to me
i hold them both in snake-veined hands

HARBOUR

for Maryka and Susanne

from toronto westward
past prairie, past rockies to
wet coast to storm
to too much drowning
you tossing ropes tossing rafts
paddling canoes howling your
lighthouse helmets flash flashing
"over here old woman swim
swim watch out for rocks"

BAGWORM

wings eyes
wind water
suddenly
dangling grey shell
autumn leaf

    or

    !

       bagworm

moth in silken case
camouflaged
debris

BATH

"she came over and cried
and cried and cried" he said
the man with the biggest bucket
he welcomed fresh hot tears
then filling his weekly tub
he bathed luxuriously
in what he had wrung
from gasping lips and trusting eyes

TOKEN

the token woman
the token in the turnstile
drops neat and useful
clank into the slot
of the efficient
subway system

occasionally
a token is twisted
and the turnstile stops
for a few moments of silence

TO WASH AWAY THE GREEN

before he said goodbye forever
he took a paintbrush
dipped it in a bucket of green
and muttering paint paint he walked
round and round dropping tart
green grapes on the floor

when he said goodbye forever
she snatched his paintbrush
dipped it in a purple pot
and painted distant mountains
one-colour sunsets, purple roses
in a goodbye sky she strung a curtain
of purple grapes and shed plump purple tears

she moved out of the darkness
in search of her flesh
terrified of the nailing of touch
and he sheltered her waking
through the fleshless night

he held the reins of storm
through the tossing night
and formed liaisons with
a still small light

in the morning she walked the streets
extravagant with greeting
as though she had inherited
a continent of childhood

PANCAKE POEM

the dough here
is heavy these days
better the buoyancy
the light tidal spray
better we trample less

A WILD THING

if you would love a wild thing
it must be after the hurts of the day
have gone out you must not cage
the swiftness as it disappears
from sight nor blame the
motorcycle or the highway
or any other sudden change of flight

home is an empty house
one enters through the broken window
if one enters at all there is to be no
running on the roofs no wild
pattering of small feet the
sunlight has fled to the piper
to the hillside to the mountain
the children have seeped
through the concrete

EARTHWORM

earth-making
prayer transforming
arid underground

sarcasm
envy
vengefulness

in such soil
earthworm labours
laboriously

CONVERSATION AFTER STORM

last night the rain
flooded the drain

can we fix the
simple valve

located here
behind the ear

HE IS FORCED TO RETIRE

having no hands now
he clings by his teeth
a mutineer
in storm-slashed seas
his breathing declaring
he still lives
and i am tossing him
my bouquets as i
shout into the storm
that i have always loved him
a blossom
without petals
naked in the night

TULIPS

as he lay in his
hospital bed
he asked
if the tulips
each bulb
i'd planted
too deeply
perhaps
had opened

i lied

i didn't know
they needed
watering

STONE MOTHER

Because she rarely laughed
Or wept or hugged almost
Never because she never
Screamed because she was stone

Her daughter also from
Volcano hewn carries
Thick liquid fire
Magma in her soul

This to legacy-laden children's
Children bequeathed this
Red currency flowing down the
Generations

A DNA of dragons who too
Will marry and transform
Flesh to stone

people stopped looking for signs
in 1910, he said when she
mentioned the red dress in the
movie the green coat
the enduring (red) moment of the
puppets the happiness (red)
down through generations
and the green (go) jacket
the child wore, green for
erasure according to the
filmmaker maybe they
didn't even think about
the colours when they were making
the movie, i'm wearing yellow
and look the light just
changed to yellow he
chuckled as they came to the
davisville subway station
between stop and go between
erasure and endurance did you
see the way the people in
the street didn't even
notice the red balloon

WE SLIP

we slip we slide we glide
one tiny thought at a time
we hardly remember how we fell

a moment's murmuring
barely a ripple
in the pond

yet in galaxies
unknown a dark
supernova

what creates more death?
your hatred of my beloved
or my hatred of you

WHAT WE ARE DOING FOR LIGHT

what we are doing for light
i do not know
or even where it is
it has become abstracted
its glow sufficiently diffuse
that is has been renamed

it is decidedly unlike
the bright memory of light
i still gladly retain

what we are doing for light
i do not know but leaves of
ficus benjamina and vine
turn greenly towards
the cold hard window from which
the light appears to be calling
though this is uncertain

PLASTIC LEAVES

some fleeting thoughts
are better untyped
unremembered unexamined
allowed to be
falling leaves
in the windy ways

alas email

THORNY POINTS

untethered and inviolable
in the sentient sea
rilke's distances and intimacies
reunited in this the
loneliest of all possible worlds

to the farthest star sending code
knowing we are dust
and crystalline connected
as are the thorny points of leaves

THIRST

drenched in salt
the thirst
for forgiveness
as a final
taste of water

here now
in the loud blaring light
at st. michael's hospital

my mother my
father my brother
wait with me
for the place
without enemies

The Splintered Moon

1967

Tongue-tied

A long black tie
With a gold spear clip
Hangs from your neck
Like a tongue which dares not wag.
You will not ever utter
Words for me to hear
Because your tongue is a black tie
And my glance a gold spear.

No Worms on My Hook

There are no worms on my hook
no bait on my line
I am inexpert
in catching fish.
The sea is the sound of my needing
the fish my objects of love
and I have no taste
for seafood.
Somewhere in the vague distance
cormorants fly
pursuing the teeming sea.
I trusted the moon to glow for a spell
and show me
the living waters
but there is only a rippling
and the moon is a splintered shell.
I trust the splintered moon
to keep me from drifting too close
to the deadly shore
to keep my eyes from seeing too much
of hungry birds.

I THINK I AM THAT FABLED PRINCESS

I think I am that fabled princess
Who could not sleep
Upon layers of soft mattresses
Because of that one hard pea beneath
And I am wondering, my love,
If we will discover
That you are that prince
Who sought me.
For if you are not
Then I am a silly saint
And you are a bed of nails.

OWNED A PAIN

I owned a pain which I kept
Beneath my ribs and thought
If I could see the pain
I would know release
But I could not because I'm not
Made of plastic so I asked the surgeon
To cut it out and let me see its shape.
He sliced me apart and I saw
The multi-pronged red wherefore within
And I bartered my bloody star
For a pointless package of peace.

NUTCRACKER

"O what a nut you are,"
You said as you broke my shell
To devour me.
I waited
To course through your bloodstream
Swish up through your heart
Trickle into your brain.
Your teeth crunched through me.
Expectantly, I entered a cavity
And then you spat me out.

OLD WOMAN

Muted
The sorrow
Hovered over
The limbless woman.
She had no arms
To wipe her tears
And no man
Fulfilled her.
Shadows
Converged over her
As silently
She watched her loves
Burning her arms.
Sometimes at the end of a trying session
No tears

No anything
Sometimes in the middle of everything
Spinning everywhere
Into nothing
A demon eye opens upon
Another demon eye
Looking in
Trying to see
And seeing nothing
Imagines blindness has finally come—
When suddenly the universe
Is a frantic leaping of eyes—
Eyes leaping
Reflecting segments—
Dots of light—
After all the trying
One wonders
Who turned the kaleidoscope—

LAUGH A LITTLE

I read somewhere that in a logging tree–blessed community
Men dance when their babies are born and
Cry when they die. For diversion they
Tie a raccoon on a floating log
And watch their dogs kill it. Like me
They fear the too-much-pain that causes death
The too-much-light that causes blindness.
Unlike me, they have learned to laugh a little.

PITY MY DRESS

Pity my dress
My red dress
Which was worn like a ribbon
Around the white explosion of my heart.
It was a fuse which fluttered
Uselessly against the blue
Contempt of your touch
And lies shredded
On the floor.
Pity my red dress.
Oh pity my red red dress.

BILLBOARD CITY

Like a black widow spider
The police car lunged out
From behind a billboard in Billboard City
To pursue
The reckless young care-for-nothing couple
Fleeing, like flies, the webs
Hung between billboards.

COMMUNICATION

You
Are swathed
In layers of silly chains
Which I may not cut
Or burn or wrench away from you
Because you love them.
To reach you
I must first say
"How beautiful are your chains today."
Then I must kneel
And tap my message on your chains
And hope
That you will hear.

IN MOOSE JAW

In compact Moose Jaw, a person
Can stand in a park
And see the library, a funeral home,
A stone shell of a church which burned
One winter night. A short block away
He can see Main Street
And the lights which say
"Go" and "Caution" and "Stop."
If not myopic he might also see
The shadowy sign that says "Pause."

SNOWFLAKE

At midnight
    Snow
        softly
            falls
Covering us
In our silent rest.
One red flake
From a luminous star
    Drops
        to earth
            and is covered
By the silent drift drift
And in the morning
A lily blooms
Where the red flake fell.

HELP ME SOMEONE

"Help me someone," I said softly
And as undramatically as possible
While standing on a small curved
Bridge over the goldfish pond.
"Help me someone," I said
As I squatted over the water.
"Help me someone," I muttered
Staring into the eyes
That stared back with a
Look of pity. I dangled
My feet over the sloping edge
And slid grumbling into
The shallow pool where bright
Goldfish swam for display.

In Memory

I wrenched you from me
I gouged your bullet eyes from my pierced throat
And tore you.
You whimpered once
Before I thrust your fluttering shreds beneath the earth
and trampled your grave.
I erected a stone memory which says "Once you lived"
and I try, I try to be kind
And kill the weeds and nourish the flowers
Because you are dead
Because you must be dead.

Loneliness

My pleading repels you
And I am far too just
To forgive.

Knew a Polite Man

I knew a polite man
Afraid to hate.
He said "I love you"
And couldn't understand
Why he coughed.

Righteous Cleansing

Here we are
Washing our hands
Cleansing of all dirt
All skin
All blood, nerve, sinew,
All bone,
Making transparent
Our clean clean
Clean hands.

Divisions

We explode ourselves
Lurch from our centres
Split ourselves into endless splinters
Releasing waves of consciousness
That swell a cohesive bind
Midst our separate parts.

We had not seen it. None of us had seen it. It was not that we were incapable of sight. But we were shielded from it. Some of us knew— most of us knew—that behind that shield it was there. Some of us chose to forget. A very few of us tore at the shield, tore wildly. But none of us fully saw.

Those of us who spent our day-long energies in battering at the shield knew that if we all, each with our ten fingernails, and two fists, clawed and grappled, if we as one endless stream of energy battered at the shield, we could see, and seeing, we could end it. But there were very few of us. And those of us who spent our day-long energy were weary at the end of our day with the futility of our scratch.

And so it came around the shield and began first with the few of us who were spending our energies battering. It came and we could not see it coming for the shield had welded to our eyes. And we lay there encompassed by it, as moment by moment it attacked us, devouring and decomposing us until nerveless and heartless we ceased and it prevailed.

We had not seen it. None of us had seen it. It was not that we were incapable of sight but we were shielded from it.

A Choice of Dreams

1974

About Japan

ANCESTORS' GRAVES IN KURAKAWA

Down down across the open sea to Shikoku
To storybook island of mist and mystery
By train and bus through remote mountain villages
Following my father's boyhood backwards
Retracing the mountain path he crossed on rice husk slippers
With his dreams of countries beyond seas beyond seas
His dreams still intact, his flight perpetual
Back down the steep red mountain path
To the high hillside grave of my ancestors
Grey and green ferns hang down
Edging my faint beginnings with shades
Maintaining muteness in a wordless flickering
The hiddenness stretches beyond my reach
Strange dew drops through cedar incense
And I greet the dead who smile through trees
Accepting the pebbles that melt through my eyes.

On Flight 401

Sea blue stewardess with celluloid limbs
Emerges through a focus of recorded words
Points one lilting fingertip
To metal compartments above
Sniffs an oxygen tube yellowy flower
Lowers a fashion show life raft

The ocean orchestrates her ballet
The air crash as distant as
The sound of the white spray

Descent into Smog

Bumpy chowder clouds our descent
Into forecast of smoke haze
Sun angles away to airport scene
The Tokyo trot
Much bowing, many bow legs
A grey kimono emerges, tightness, anxiety—
My aunt has helmetitis, or is it
Just a temporary helmet she puts on
When something has to be done—
Like walking under ladders
Standing in hard hat areas
Meeting North American strangers—
She asks hard hat questions:
What's your name, girl? Curiosa?
Cursiosa? Schedule, purpose
What's your game?
Home is where the heart is, I feel
Which is an open question
These wounding days.
She escorts me through black exhaust
Hurtling smog, open toilet smells
Jerky conversation, I cut the automatic
And turn to manual breathing, watch the
Red alert in my temple and
Try to adjust.

STREET CORNER, TOKYO

A duster of hippies
Flowers of plastic bags gripped to their noses
Inhale themselves off the island
To places hazy as drift cloud
Plastered with paint thinner

A farmer totters by on geta
Swallows his sakë and is swallowed
Into the bloodstream, a droplet
Dripping into the world's liver

An artist paints a dusty tree
Assigns his signature
To a falling leaf

ZEN GRAVEYARD

Thick night mist
Mountainside, stone ghosts, graves
Rising in steps into trees
Strange familiarity
Small girl once upon a time
Red and white kimono, short hair
Not here perhaps but somewhere
A wild boar perhaps, perhaps not
Waterfall, a sound not unlike a violin
Bell tone of insect, praying mantis nearby
Curled coloured snails on mossy trees—
To have to stand alone here
In this almost place when
Once upon a time, perhaps—

ON HEARING JAPANESE HAIKU

Throat blossoms to sounds
Sama zama no mono
Stirrings in the sandy fibres of my flesh
And these ancient fingers
Gardening

A TEMPO

Lost in a maze of corridors
With a useless map
Streets the width of hallways
And basin-size backyard gardens
Bow-legged women churn the
Everywhere falling dust
Brown air brown arms brown earth
A piano player plays a Bach fugue
With the piano
Almost on the sidewalk
A patchy rooster
Squats in a cramped cage

GLANCES

At first glance I am in a no-shout, no-spank
Network of sensitivity training course graduates,
The only reprimand being "Everyone is watching you."
Fierce eyes, fearful eyes are more than enough
And shame is the public watchdog.

At second glance I notice tiny pockmark scars
On the back of a lady's hand and remember
That peculiar old Japanese punishment
Of setting a Sen-Sen–sized square to smoulder
And burn a brand on the naughty child's skin—
A strange code of barely discernible public glances
And private barbarisms—a constant inconsistency
And multi-standard code of behaviour.

By the fifth and sixth glances I come to a tangle
Of subtleties, stomach ulcers and suicides
And I surface for air in an art gallery.
On one wall hangs an outline of a pot in red
With the English word POT printed in green.
A thin line borders the picture
With dimensions in neat Roman numerals
Marked in the lower right corner.

At first glance I am drained of subtlety
But by the fifth and sixth glances
I am fleeing the art gallery
To watch a tea ceremony
Where guests empty their minds
As they empty the contents of ancient rustic tea bowls.
At first glance the tea ceremony
Seems a tedious discipline fit for the old.

This Is a Clearing

This is a clearing
There is the forest
This is the forest
There is the clearing.
My gentle relatives are standing in dark sunlight
Whispered about with monumental propriety
Gathering on the occasion of a wedding
To impale and dismember a missing relative
Chanting a creed "We belong. We belong."
I stand on the edge
If I enter the forest I am lost
If I enter the clearing I am still lost
I move in a direction
Chanting a creed "We belong. We belong."
A large tree cracks

ON MEETING THE CLERGY OF THE HOLY CATHOLIC CHURCH IN OSAKA

Heralded into a belly-swelling bladder-bloating banquet
Where the excessive propriety is hard on the digestion
Elegant ladies in kimonos and holy men with holier manners
Bow and re-bow in strict pecking order
Munch the meal and mouth polite belching and
Rush at flood tide to the integrated toilet
Where men still proper and black suited in a row
Stand toes out and eyes down in syncopated gush
While ladies in kimonos mince by without blush or bellow
And I follow snuffling to hide a guffaw though
Why I should laugh—which reminds me
At the Osaka zoo my friend kept pointing out
The peeing fox and the baboon's purple bum and such
Asking how to say these things in English
And I tried to explain about the odd Canadians
Who have no bread-and-butter words
To describe these ordinary things.

FOR THE ANNUAL SERVICE OF THANKS THAT KYOTO WAS SPARED THE BOMB

For the fact that this temple was not bombed
And these dragons still stand guard—
For this network of lanes on the city's edges
Shaded by ancient trees
For this pre-Meiji pond and its family of rocks
This still living and aging thatch-roofed house
For Kinkakuji and Ginkakuji and countless wooden buildings
For these and other treasures still preserved
We give thanks, o military strategists
And wish a happy unbirthday to you Kyoto,
Pollyanna city of grace and gratitude.
A few miles away in Hiroshima
The wide boulevard in front of Peace Park
Is jammed on International Peace Day
With a new generation of students
Who feel they know what to say.

THE CHICKEN KILLING

Down the dusty country lane
Along drying rice propped in lines like soldiers on parade
And blue-pantalooned people in the distance pantomiming—
Two men standing, three crouched in ritual stance
Sweat cloths around foreheads, open undershirts, black cloth boots
One with knife, one grinning toothless—
Plump white fluttering held feet first
Conveniently drains its veins as it struggles
Then flung aside, leaps through the air—
I walk past down the trembling road
Tasting the sound of dusty feet and
Feeling on my neck the slight saltiness of a question—
I am dangling feet first from the sky
—Perhaps if I do not struggle—

PUBLIC BATH

Daily to the ofuro
With basin, soap, towel and thirty-five yen
With neighbours strangers and friends
To boil away altogether
All together in the bath
And with wash cloth rolled tight
As hard ball pumice stone
Scrape and scrub each other's backs
Already lobster red from steam
Squat and flob flob with soap
And splash and soak again
Till steam and dumpling soft
We merge as one warm vat
Of boiled jelly fish
All our offensive scabs and irritations
Rolled off in communal banter.
Would that this could be exported home
And politicians and businessmen and sons
Could meet together in the public bath
To batter and scrub each other raw
And dissolve the ills of the day
And my frozen neighbours in suburbia
Grannies and babies and mothers
And children all wrapped in skin
Could melt at the end of their day.

SATURDAY NIGHT IN OSAKA

Strolling along the stretching Saturday night streets of Osaka
Between Osaka station and the dark corner of the YWCA
Jostled by mini car and multi-legged man
In narrow lane of lantern light and noise
Screeching brakes of unoiled bicycles
Pachinko parlours, glowing purple escalators
With my Japanese face in my dragon lady disguise
English like a dagger in my teeth
Flashing out against lonely challenging men
"Be my friend, Miss? Have some tea?"
Shrug. (I don't speak Japanese anyway, kid.)
I saunter back to the safety of the Y
And glumly brush my fangs with toothpaste
Like a million other antiseptic inhibited biddies
Who fear to look ridiculous or worse
And for the rest of the evening
Thumb through a Japanese-English dictionary
And listen to the man in the next alley
As he directs the traffic of a swaggering Saturday night
Shouting "Orai Orai Orai" (All right. All right.)
Among the centipedes and dragonflies and exploding neon lights.

DAY OF THE BRIDE

The day of the bride dawns
Through layers of white plaster skin
And multi-sashed kimono
Head made huge by lacquered hair—
She is swept ashore in her glass bottle
White and tight as a folded paper message
Eyes hidden in a swirl of green boughs.
She moves like a mannequin
Manoeuvred by centuries of ceremony
Under the weight of speech and incantation
A wail of priests and watching families
Beside rows of low tables
With small triangles of paper
Congratulatory slits of squid and curls of seaweed.
Then kneeling at the bend of a fresh memory
She is discarded by her heavy day
And is plunged into the twentieth century
Tiny apartment daily stream
As a barely visible
Folded paper speck

Rush Hour Tokyo

Pelted shapeless in rush hour crush
As in a whash mash mochi making
A mad cab exhaust spot
Bicycle pedestrian car cart jostling
Hip to bumper, wheel to toe
Police whistle siren scream political
Speech radio singer neon I blur
Into this excess of faceless flesh rushing
Round this blender of glazed eyes—
Particle waves of people
Whip at typhoon speed past ticket takers
The world's most accurate mechanical men
And pummel up subway systems
Spew onto streets and platforms
Where demons within demons within demons
Riot for release or finale
Like staccato repetitions in frenzied fugues
Locked in a constant crescendo—
Canada oh my home and native land
Give me land lots of land don't
Fence don't fence me in—

Night in a Boat between Beppu and Kobe

At least three hundred men and five women
In the lower section of this rocking boat
Squeezed body to body on the thrumming floor
Some men fully dressed in underwear
Drinking sakë, playing cards and singing
Some already snoring open mouthed
Stiff on their backs beside each other
I squinch into my corner and lie down
Too curious to sleep too proper to be comfortable
The question of the unalert moment
Propping open my east-west eyes
A man's foot is on my buttock help
But he seems to be asleep
And I am watchtower
Witnessing on a busy corner
Sleepwalking with a pamphlet in my hand
That says Awake, Lick the crust from your eyelids
Watch and wait (it's a sightseeing trip)
I begin the taking off and putting on of masks
Smiling carefully at the man on my other side
And frowning at the demons dancing
Gleeing to my bright dark imaginings
By morning I am in a stupor
Having dramatized my corner all night
But can only report that there is no action
In having a strange man's foot on one's buttock
In a crowded overnight boat in Japan.
On the deck and in the first class cabins
Other passengers have been viewing
What some say is the world's
Most scenic inland sea.

Newspaper Item: Student Suicide

In soot silence, bamboo grows
Tree surgeons discuss the cause of wood rot
Pines point crooked arms to the sky

Rain drops the sky down in grey pieces and
Darkness moves with the urgency of flight
From a bad dream

Every day
The newspaper reports
A bad dream

Tomorrows were mountaintops
Sculptured pines
And wind-pruned asymmetry

A student went chestnut picking
And heard the "mim mim"
Of an autumn cicada.

DWARF TREES

Out of the many small embarrassments of the day
Grew a miniature personality
Leafing itself gingerly in whatever genuine smile
It recognized in the thick undergrowth.
Dwarf trees planted in a fertile gentleness
Beside lush vegetation and sheltering green fans
Grew angular and stunted in a constant adjustment to cutting.
Horns of new growths sprouted
To bleed into warts and tiny anxieties.
Glances of disapproval felt as sharply
As salivating fangs tore at limbs.
Men developed into twisted sculptures of endurance
Bowing and smiling in civilized anger
And old women pruned daily into careful beauty
Glanced away in a cultivated shyness
Hiding smiles with humpbacked hands
Symbolizing by small gestures
Tiny treasures from a hidden childhood.

Lost Man at the Tourist Information Centre

Wide-eyed and childlike the lost one comes
Bulbous-nosed Australian, outstandingly fat
Flailing his stubby wings at all the strange
Bobbing creatures in his way.
Booms at the prim hostess
"I've been in Japan a fortnight
And haven't eaten a good Australian meal
I'm almost starving to death."
Japanese blinks at the bulk in front.
No mirth.
Clucking efficiency she flutters
On her perch at the Lost and Found booth
Roots through directories for the choicest grub
Bobs and bows the waddler on his way
Into the mad taxi traffic
Of the Ginza barnyard
Where he bellows like a baby ox
Lost in a forest of fragility
And intensely earnest jack-in-a-boxes
Doing abstract choreography.

SCHOOL IN THE WOODS

North Korean school in Kyoto woods, sports day
Blue-white uniformed young people,
Military music, red star in white circle
A poster of a soldier wielding a long gun
Another of a toothy U.S. devil
Bayoneting an oriental man

A small boy in front of me eats a rice ball
And watches me with a careful stare
It is an autumn day in Kyoto
Full of tiny coloured maple leaves

Back home, some mother glimpses
Bayonets in the air, turns off the TV
Tucks her child into bed

Moon over Uchiko

9:00 p.m. evening lullaby and gong
Half hymn, half child's play song
Over this mountain village
Cicadas and crickets chirp whirr
Acorns drop down with soft thuds—
I slip through softly sliding doorways
Of matchstick wood and paper
To where my aunt in grey kimono
Sits in a rock garden by a pond
Beneath a white moon without hint of footprint.
Shuffling pigeon toed my aunt of much bowing
Descends upon my feet with great graciousness
Clutches my arms and clings parallel to earth
Suspended in the ether of my deciding
"Stay longer. Stay longer. Stay. Stay."
She opens for me her collection of memories
—My father as a child gathering cow dung for the garden
—My grandmother accused of farting in school
and weeping in a tub for a day—
She tugs me towards her dry hollows
And I am deformed with etiquette
As my plastic arms encircle her
And melt in the heat of her tears.
The steel beam in my back cracks
As she leans heavily crying and sighing.
I begin the countdown. Words to prop her
A cane for her to clutch. "Dear Aunt
I am beginning to learn how better to lie."
She bends double as I depart in a gust of metal
Rocketing the willowy trees bare in her October garden.

Rooting for the smooth grey fish
Being hooked and snared by laughing child
And powerless in the cool grey weather
To leap out of one element into another
Wishing only to avoid the death
Of being hooked on my gills by some cosmic child
And gleefully serenaded into a pebbly blackness
Of some gourmet's solar intestines—
Saying with vehemence I am a fish
And will die the death of a cold grey fish
Near my familiar mountain waterfall
But even here fishermen dangle
Worms on hooks into the stream of my peace
To pull me up into the rare foreign air.
Above the surface of my sky
Pure white seagulls circle
And I know that if I bite
It is for a devouring and an end
To the swift flash of my dark
Sporting body beneath the bumpy waves
But what does it matter to rot here or there
If I cannot will away this child
And the expansive smiling of his father.

In round round rooms of our wanderings
Victims and victimizers in circular flight
Fact pursuing fact
Warning leaflets still drip down
On soil heavy with flames,
Black rain, footsteps, witnessings—

The Atomic Bomb Memorial Building:
A curiosity shop filled with
Remnants of clothing, radiation sickness,
Fleshless faces, tourists muttering
"Well, they started it."
Words jingle down
"They didn't think about us in Pearl Harbor"
They? Us?
I tiptoe round the curiosity shop
Seeking my target
Precision becomes essential
Quick. Quick. Before he's out of range
Spell the name
America?
Hiroshima?
Air raid warnings wail bleakly
Hiroshima
Morning.
I step outside
And close softly the door
Believing, believing
That outside this store
Is another door .

INSOMNIA IN A RYOKAN

What? No sound down the corridor?
No multiplicity of foot falls
Flap flap slippered slap
Or patter thud of plastic sole?
Only this foreign wooden floor
Only this faint echo of radio, TV, faraway drama
Flamenco dancers in dreams
Hints of snoring through hotel walls
What more can one ask?
A leap to a naked drum beat?
A primitive frenzy of touch?
One can insist on footsteps
One can insist on dancing
Look, the midnight can take shape
Slender fingerlings of dancing
Can cavort down corridors
Hah!
I'll leap into your snoring
Shout out my English subtitles
"Let me in!"
If you could understand my fairy tales

Holy Name Orphanage and Fukuse Byoin

The Holy Name Orphanage
Where an old blue-hooded nun
Part eagle, part fish, feeds a baby
Her skinny intellectual hand
Holding a heavy spoon
She jerks his face frontwards
Shovel, jerk, shovel
He vomits finally
Small streams of mushy yellow
Down her blue skirt to the floor
She rises taller than she is
Avenging angel marching out
The baby watching her
And no longer intent on watching me.
I leave in an hour to visit
Fukuse Byoin at the foot of Mount Fuji—
A man skull faced and eaten away
After twenty years of Hansen's disease
Lies with sightless eyeballs perpetually bared
Bedridden, force fed, a gaping mouth
Uttering sounds in his constant night
A Hallowe'en mask
I leave in an hour again
Walk the haunted city streets
Lady Macbeth, graduate tourist

FLOWER ARRANGER

Among the weedy steel structures
And frenetic flowering of factories
I found a blind flower arranger
In a sketch of a room
Dipping a drop of water
Onto an opening petal
Of a tiny not quite flowering bud.
With his fingertips
He placed gentleness in the air
And everywhere among the blowing weeds
He moved with his outstretched hands
Touching the air
With his transient dew.

BLACK SKIRT OF MOUNT FUJI IN RAIN

Almost late for the Tomei bus to Nagoya
Spot the one empty seat and sit down
By the bleary-eyed man the others had shunned
He takes out his Suntory whisky, peels off
The plastic top, nudges me tentatively.
We travel on through several stages of misunderstanding
Me, anxious to see the countryside
And listening to the recorded announcements.
"Mount Fuji to the left" the voice says.
I peer out the window. Pouring rain.
The mountain exists in my imagination.
The next announcement. "I'm sorry
When you are in such a hurry
To have to stop for refuelling."
A lunchgirl arrives calling
"Bother is being done. Is lunch desired?"
Politeness all over this apologetic country
And I had to get old Suntory.
I decide to do a Mount Fuji
And obliterate myself in mist.
"Yes" I say in English to the nudger
"What would you like?"

GEISHA

Invitations
dangle
from strings
like small
gem bead
curtains

eyes downcast
she steps through
and on her cheeks
are pink
flower
bruises

she paints
her sunsets
to match
his watching
and washes away
her mornings

HANGNAIL

Wondering about the importance of this hangnail
And its power over this massive hulk
Which dangles tenuously from its ledge
And this shuffling mass of a hangnail
From which the universe protrudes—
A hug might help
But I can't feel any cosmic arms
Nor earthly ones—
While walking I stepped on a giant moth
And in the long moment of its dying
All the accummulated injustices
Of squashed and battered bugs
Sacrificed on windshields
And sprayed to oblivion
Poured out of its eloquent wings
In one long fluttering—
And now the blood throbs in my thumb—
Attempting to atone the foot's misadventure?
Offering a salve of forgetfulness
To assuage my guilt?
An eye for an apple, a tooth for a pick
Kill the bugs if they make you sick—
The hangnail drones on interpreting itself
In the maze of my notions of justice
Which hang on as tenaciously and irritatingly
As a hangnail thread.

Dream after Touring the Tokyo Tokei

Electronic baby born to be
Guide in clock manufacturing hospital
Son of General Secretary of Resurrection
With a white bib on cold steel chest
Comes sliding squealing into this world
Ready to perform his single task
And guides me, ancient earthling
Through metal spot after metal spot
Where oil, like blood, alive, is flowing and
Small steel birds beep through the air
Carrying messages of cheer to the ill—
"Behold, before you were born I was here."
I reach out and am electrocuted
And the steel baby within me leaps—
Oh be born quickly before my flesh is Sarah grey
That I might see the shape of ancient promise

We step outside to Tokyo twentieth century
Seeds of slaves drift down from factory windows
And settle in the branches of dwarf trees
Settle on metal ledges and in the streets
Drop like confetti over the rose garden
And inside the bonnet of an opening rose
On the wrinkled old woman face of the bud
Stands a stiff black beetle on steely legs
An ancient wedding procession begins
In the dusty rose garden by the Tokyo Tokei.

GODDESS OF MERCY

Autumn and not one leaf
On grey white sand, constant ripple
Of pebbly sea rock garden
The Goddess of Mercy rests her bronze ankle
On her knee, unmoving and perfect.
I slash the air like a medieval executioner
At a mosquito swooping past my face
And across the sand sea of eternity
Into the safety of the thick moss
My black blood in its belly.
Across the smoggy sky, two jets criss-cross
From the highway a whine of traffic
Swells and fades

GIRLS IN THE GINZA

Bleach me brown or bleach me blonde
The Japanese girl demands
Surrounded by Caucasian mannequins
Mocking oriental beauty.
She begs the plastic surgeon man
To snip the muscles of her slitty eyes
Lift her nose, plump her breasts—
False eyelashes and latest fashions on
She walks around the Ginza
Not quite who she wants to be
Her thick black hair rusting
Under the peroxide rain

GIFT GIVING AND OBLIGATION

Note from the lonely spaces:
Beware the kindness of the smother places
Where you are offered gift on gift.
Refuse carefully. Watch the eyes.
If they dart suddenly away from your glance
Smile and acknowledge the testing.
If the eyes murmur pleasure at your refusal
Refuse yet more profusely
Smiling with acceptance
Then condescend finally
Allowing and acknowledging
The superiority of gift giving.
Walk away burdened with an obligation
To continue exchanging for eternity
Complete with rituals of accumulating thankfulness
Or leave swiftly in the night
Before your neck is fastened with a whispering,
"Weight, weight, I love you."
Swim from the seaweed and strangulation
Westward to another island.

CHILD EICHMANN

The orders were to kill the kittens
And obedience was the first commandment.
He took the first, still sac enclosed
A slippery blackness in his kitten-size palm
And drowned it in a pail of water
Felt its pawing with needle-thin scratchings
Watched it swimming, mewing, gaping—
Life comes, goes, mouths open, close,
The small sounds are buried in the night's
Darkness and wild dreaming. "Okaasan!"
She blames the persimmons and squats him
Over the open toilet which has not yet
Been cleaned by the monthly manure collector.
The smell from his bowels fills the house.

Bamboo Broom

At the Shinto shrine
Grey green stone lanterns
Scowling Chinese lion dogs
Protecting against irreverence and intrusion
Triangular tiny white porcelain foxes
Grains of rice placed at the feet
Of the rice god, Oinari-san
A record playing "Dinah won't you blow—"
A woman tossing a ten yen piece
Into a wooden box, bowing her head
Clapping her hands twice
Moss, water, tiny plum trees
PEACE cigarettes on the path
Another brand called HOPE
(Is there one called GOODWILL?)
A woman with a bamboo broom
Sweeping the ground
A tour of schoolchildren
In navy blue English uniforms
Crowding in past the lion dogs
(swish swish swish)

At Maruyama Park, Kyoto

Up stone steps to dark temple at night
A wail of flickering lights around stone statues
Centuries of looking down
Water drips, moss clings
A tiny brown frog leaps
Splash
Into a pool

AT SHINJUKU PARK, NOVEMBER 19

Through the park
In autumn, warm leaf time
With transient foot
It being time to go home
Time, swear, to go home
And some loudspeaker plays
"Auld Lang Syne"
Yanking a raindrop out of nowhere.
We trudge through the song
Carrying the ocean with us.
Above us, seagulls cross
On a path of splashing waves
Brushing aside whatever spray
Clings to their wings
Their feathers filled with the buoyancy
Of those who love them.
Little point in delaying departure
Now the time to go has come
In the middle of this dance
In this autumn morning
I cling to my flight
While the rain
Gushes over my wings
And my goodbye face

EARLY MORNING STAGE

A messy city
Early morning and traffic whine mosquito whine
Toilet smell, cricket and dog sounds
Corrugated cardboard sheets
Oddly, a cow mooing? a rooster crowing?
The mosquito jabs my arm
I pull myself out of the heavy futon
Step over tatami to hallway
Slip on slip off slippers
Cloth slippers for hall
Plastic slippers for toilet
Squat fetal fashion over the flushless hole.
Through the floor-level window vent
The sounds of feet pass
Outside in the pre-dawn grey and constant smog
Early morning scuttlers disappear
Pigeons flutter with the debris
A man with a fist full of red flowers
Urinates against a bush
A girl with an easel paints a school building
A loudspeaker above the school door plays
The "What a Friend We Have in Jesus" march
Bicycles with primitive brakes screech
Ladies hang futons over railings
A roast potato man
Pulls his wooden cart and calls
"Yaki imo" through his scratchy loudspeaker—
I remember that corner of Tokyo
But now I open my eyes
To a suburban white-walled house in Ottawa
Early morning and a long silence
As if the curtain has just gone up

Or down and something electrifying has just happened
Or is about to happen and the day has begun
Or ended. It is up to me to decide
I am director producer playwright or
Actress on stage needing
Laughing lessons and I'm thinking
Of firing her. The audience has disappeared
And the walls intrude.
The mail truck crunches by.

Trunk in the Attic

Rummaging through the old metal trunk in
The attic above the church hall in Coaldale, Alberta—
The trunk which travelled with us
Through the World War II evacuation of Japanese
From the West Coast—filled then with dishes
Dresses and assorted treasures
And now only half full of baby dresses,
An old tablecloth, invitations to dinner Xmas 1915—
My white-haired mother hands me
A deep purple kimono bought
In some vaguely remembered girlhood
Of apple-shaped pears and sweet chestnuts
And utterly unabandoned babies
Asleep on their mothers' backs—
I take the memories from her tapered fingers
Fold her hands which no longer cling
Close the lid of the trunk.
The sharp whiff of mothballs fades from the room
And she turns to climb down the stairs
One step at a time
Rubbing the mucus steadily
From her cataract-covered eyes.

Forest Creatures

WHEN I WAS A LITTLE GIRL

When I was a little girl
We used to walk together
Tim, my brother who wore glasses,
And I, holding hands
Tightly as we crossed the bridge
And he'd murmur "You pray now"
—being a clergyman's son—
Until the big white boys
Had kicked on past.
Later we'd climb the bluffs
Overhanging the ghost town
And pick the small white lilies
And fling them like bombers
Over Slocan.

BREEZES

The weeping willow sways low
In the breeze it seems to brush
The tops of those distant bushes
Sensuously in my one-dimensional
Perception. Once I imagined
I knew so well the meaning
Of your careful words brushing
My mind gently with a nearness
Now I see how distant
The bushes are I still
Would paint them touching.

WHAT DO I REMEMBER OF THE EVACUATION

What do I remember of the evacuation?
I remember my father telling Tim and me
About the mountains and the train
And the excitement of going on a trip.
What do I remember of the evacuation?
I remember my mother wrapping
A blanket around me and my
Pretending to fall asleep so she would be happy
Though I was so excited I couldn't sleep
(I hear there were people herded
Into the Hastings Park like cattle.
Families were made to move in two hours
Abandoning everything, leaving pets
And possessions at gunpoint.
I hear families were broken up
Men were forced to work. I heard
It whispered late at night
That there was suffering) and
I missed my dolls.
What do I remember of the evacuation?
I remember Miss Foster and Miss Tucker
Who still live in Vancouver
And who did what they could
And loved the children and who gave me
A puzzle to play with on the train.
And I remember the mountains and I was
Six years old and I swear I saw a giant
Gulliver of Gulliver's Travels scanning the horizon
And when I told my mother she believed it too
And I remember how careful my parents were
Not to bruise us with bitterness
And I remember the puzzle of Lorraine Life

Who said "Don't insult me" when I
Proudly wrote my name in Japanese
And Tim flew the Union Jack
When the war was over but Lorraine
And her friends spat on us anyway
And I prayed to the God who loves
All the children in his sight
That I might be white.

Chain Necklace

In my dream my mother wore
A necklace of small chains
Like a choker round her long neck
Which emphasized her beauty
And her swan-like gracefulness
And in real life she made
Her choices, wore her chains
Kept her cygnets in the
Ugly barnyard world
Told me constantly to be
Gentle and to wear
The heavy chains with joy
But I grew squat and goose-like
And pick and jab my noose
At every chance.
My daughter takes the chains
Of daisies that I make
And twines them round our arms
But when I step aside
I learn that daisies bleed
Then slowly turn to steel.

WOODTICK

The spring day the teen on his bike slanted his Caucasian eyes
At my eight-year-old beautiful daughter
And taunted gibberish
I was eight-years-old and the Japs were
Enemies of Canada and the big white boys
And their golden-haired sisters who
Lived in the ghost town of Slocan
Were walking together, crowding me
Off the path of the mountain, me running
Into the forest to escape
Into the pine brown and green lush dark
And getting lost and fearing woodticks
Which burrowed into your scalp beneath
Thick black hair follicles and could only be
Dug out by a doctor with hot needles—
Fearing sudden slips caused by melting snow
And steep ravines and the thick silence of
Steaming woods and cobwebs, so listening
For the guiding sound of their laughter
To lead me back to the path and
Following from a safe distance unseen
Till near the foot of the mountain
Then running past faster than their laughter
Home, vowing never to go again to the mountain
Alone—and Deidre whispers to walk faster
Though I tell her there are no
Woodticks in Saskatoon.

FOREST CREATURES

On this street there lives a little dark girl
A little dark girl with an orange coat
Black stockings and new shiny black shoes
Running to school through the mangled forest
One shiny new shoe flung away
By laughing boys with tiger faces—
Later my black-haired daughter
Comes dancing home both shoes on
Replying "Well she cheats when we play."
But tomorrow they are all together
Blue eyes, black hair, orange coat, tiger boys,
Skipping double dutch in the driveway
Colours all blending in a buttery chant.

SNAKES

Suddenly in the woods a
Green and yellow snake as if he
Slithered down my back
A moving rope of wind slinking an instant
Barber shop sign round my spine
And as I clambered out of the woods—
Suddenly on the path a presence
Of children, one fearful whispering
"Chinese" and the other
Moving swiftly past—

TRANSPLANT

It's a matter of being
Uprooted by this gardener secretly
In the long dark night of my
Growing and planted in the
Sudden noon day trembling
Green house touch of his
Hands. It's a matter of blossoms
Exploding through the roots of my
Slow black hair and being
Trapped by the tendrils

WATERFALL

In the space behind the waterfall
With that white sound background
On the cool rocks—
We lay there
Last night the pupils of your eyes
Were as large as Easter morning
The tunnel leading underground
And we were crouching
In the cave of our eyes
Our hands, water, flowing
Over the rock contours
Our hands, wings, blowing
The tombstone we
Heard the sound of sunrise
The flesh sound of word

PRAY MY MANTIS

Dread this morning early and no
More sleeping. Awake to
Heavy summer tuneless song
The voice of mourning
Pray my lord mantis it
Is not so our green
Limbs an instant and the
Screeching birds over all

FLOWERING

The whole approach seems
Too young somehow
I mean—not because
Nudity is offensive, indeed
There is a glory in bronze
But I resent your insistence
That all must be tested by
The fire of our hot eyes.
Love flowers
When we deal gently
With shadows.

We Were Talking About Stability

finally all the deceptions—
cloud, flight, departure
and i have said i do not
trust anymore but what
do i believe on this
plane? above? these clouds?
we are, i know, walking
on meringues and broken
egg shells, aren't we,
and trampling it all
solid—

FINALLY THAT THERE IS

no corner left in which to hide
the mouse, the cat
the empty room
the one defence left
is not to move at all
not to write
not to think
not to send you this letter

finally in the cat's jaws
i remember the secret door
listen for your tunnelling
realize finally that
you are the cat
you are the mouse
you are the room without doors
you are the secret tunnel

finally this fatal defence
fangs sharp with belief
back arched and clawing
the heart's walls

TEA PARTY

When birds dance for instance
Heads cocked, wings spread
Leaping back and forth, tearing turf
Instead of feathers

And we are polite and elegant
Sipping tea with steady hands
The wings beating beneath
Our ribs behind our eyes

FIREBUGS

We seemed to be seeking a
Mutual mugging, a double
Disintegration, we leapt over
The hanging cliff together
And fell with slow tenderness
In a consuming ballet an invisible
Hummingbird of hands and we talked
Of falling stars and the
Natural deaths on the rocks below
Our eyes faltering on the corniness
As the rocks shifted just enough
To show us the centre of the earth
Was still on fire and our soft
Avalanche gained bewilderment.

That We Might Not Cling

a bird, you said, notice
how efficient it is twitching there
on the branch, chirping, eating and
crapping at the same time. and
disappearing too, i said

October 3

we were watching the ducks
in the middle of the river
the current swift as our blood
and the ducks
looking as if they were
not moving at all

we were as if
standing still watching the ducks
and he said
"should we fly south"

i said "yes"
and he talked about other things
while i stared at
the idiotic ducks

later there were
no ducks later
still no
river

SOUTH OF FLIN FLON, HIGHWAY 10

Two men fighting at Cranberry Portage
On the sidewalk, Sunday morning,
Choking, shouting, a silent crowd gathering,
Streaky-faced children on café steps
Watching their elders
What else is there to do? Question
Do you tell it the way it is?
What is the way it is?
We in the car going by slowly to watch
The out of time story, we the out of place people.
Later on the highway we see a porcupine
Snout in air, outraged quills still quivering
Question. Is it dead? Is it suffering?
We say we don't know and keep driving
The car gradually picking up speed
Fleeing the weekend questions
The streaky-faced children in the back seat
Finally growing silent and falling asleep.

Beach Poem

Walking in warm knee-deep water
Watching tiny waves inside of waves
Inside of waves from hands and legs and
Bodies and boats and breeze
And making flat splashes, water leaping
In fat silver flashes to round circle bubbles
To float and pop and disappear forever
And repeating the flash and watching
The coming and going water pattern
And not seeing the round bald man
Who suddenly comes and splashes
And playfully grins yellow teeth
And grunts startlingly like a pig
And the water murky around him
And small pearly waters dripping
All around all around and I wish
I had a curly tail but sadly it is only forked

Rain Dance

Pestalozzi rainbow children in June storm
Deviant as ducklings in a chicken coop
Wings slapping naked skin
Under the window watching wire mesh
Hi yi yi yi Hi yi yi yi
Let it rain down let it rain
Clog the drains with dancing
Here are ark dwellers, dove senders
Mad as Noah

Porcupine

This is the way you are, Porcupine
I would wish you were otherwise
Gentle animal
Barricaded
Against my touch

NET

wait the net just
a minute why your
hands my throat your eyes my
fingers wait it's a mistake all
this i only meant (hear me)
FRIENDSHIP
hear me your
hands a
sieve my words the
gills (hush) is it
only this (yes) i can
offer the
waves
the fins

THE GIRL WHO CRIED WOLF

"I love you" she said
"I do not lie."
She showed him the slash in her arm.
"How can you sit there" she asked
"Just sit there sit there."
"Because" he said "it is the way of wolves."

Child Painting

A pink cloud, only
"At night" his black brush says
"You cannot see it
But it's still there moving
And tomorrow perhaps hail"
His brush grows roots
Flings branches skywards
A long black tree
Searching shapes
Enclosing clouds in a
Growing large
Black bird
"Tell me about your
Picture, Bobby."
Words are stones to birds in flight
His elbows move like wings.

Registration

Registration day was
Something like labour
All that waiting and
Walking and pushing and
Having finally registered
In one (1) ONE! course
I feel I've given birth
Successfully to a hamster

TOM CAT

The Tom cat comes calling Fluff
Meowering at the window
Though Fluff now hard ballooned
And weight flopping can't
Prance the cat call game
Fluff flops eyes narrowing contentment
Ignoring the ill-timed serenade
Contemplating the kittens squishing her belly
And Tom trots off eventually

An alley cat, Tom and a piper's son
Eager for thievery with his tail
A swish this side of laughter
He shakes down fresh alleys
To a new pet shop kitten
The dry water velvet cling
Pussy cat fur of her
Curling round his thirsty skin
Raised in an alley of alternatives
Tom trots on continually

Biting Silences

The neat way they eat
Indicates nobility
But occasionally
They dine with pack rats
Fangs at the table are fine
Sometimes.

Afterwards, they burn my letters
In the fireplace.

Ants Are Taking Over

Ants are taking over my world
Woe to dancing grasshoppers
Beneath the concrete slab of my face
Ants are building tunnels
Neatly stock-piling
Small grains of knowledge
At day's end the ants
Mount their mounds
Burrow through the pupils of my eyes
And giggle
At which point the ant smasher
With his midnight heel
Gouges a red hole in my concrete face.

Waiting Room

WAITING

A very quiet
                very quiet ticking
In the room where the child
Stays by the window
Watching
While outside innumerable snow feathers
Touch melt
                touch melt
                            touch melt

WAITING ROOM

Midnight and the monks
Move down the corridor
"Dona nobis pacem"
The elves in the forest
The leaves breathing
Doctors, nurses
White in the moonlight—
Beneath a toppled toadstool
Clusters of ants carry white eggs
Struggle through collapsing tunnels

Three Dreams

1.

i rub the toy train on my sleeve
dusting it carefully
moving its wheels et cetera
wondering where the motor is
where the genie is

2.

on board the ship we find there are
many ways to cut the apple
to make the exquisite tiny ridges
for a special apple dessert
it's the sort of thing that belongs
in a world without wars.

3.

she looks out the window
seeing the fire of the wars coming
we rush outside to rid ourselves
of poison. we vomit profusely
and make brown dung mounds
and this is our sole preparation

the day of lies approaches
if we tell all before the enemy comes
he will find the village emptied
and only the wind in the temple left
waiting to do him battle

how shall i tell of apples
in a world of wars

ALL THE TREES COLOURED WERE

all the trees coloured were
bird full and song ready to move
the forests alive with leaf swish and
ballet shoes on when suddenly
the "no" storm fell cloud down
and curtain heavy i
cocoon the dark

           grope
my fingernails black
the strange—
everywhere the strange
no colours left—

ROOSTER

Spear or smirk what does it matter
What the weapon is the wounds
Need tending need tenderness
What does it matter where the
Error lies when they
Come these days they
Come at once a
Rush of wounds and tenderness
With the rooster calling
His feet rooted in the night
His wings in the morning this is
Still the time
To forgive, to be forgiven

Acceptance

a goliath of thoughts
about truth and schizophrenia
and your cowardice and my
judging you—i discover
david's stone was an avalanche
connected to this simple thing—
your truths are not mine and
it's okay

DEAR EUCLID

Moon announces at the end of my dream
"Dear Euclid
I am indescructible
I am star."

July. Thursday. 1971. New York.
From the airplane we drop
Ant powder on entire continents of bloodless ants
Like rain on Dolly's parade
The tickertape confetti turning ash white
It's just a matter of time now
The cars crawling like paramecia
In drying drops

9:40. Sleepwalk into hot muggy New York
Stew people leaping from pot to pot
Swim through stop lights, computer talk
Please detach and retain this stub
For your personal use detach please
Your personal stub and retain your use
Do not fold staple or mutilate
Mold not do stupilate faple and
Give name age serial number
Ride up elevator. Salute. All that is
Tinier than Tom Thumb is not human
It is written on the screen of our understanding.
East Side Clinic. 11 :00 a.m.

I had the choice—the dreamer has
A choice of dreams—I have
The choice still to turn about
In this tight tunnel ant corridor

Carrying my huge white ant egg
With all these other worker ants
Our antennae flashing urgency
The ground shaking our Soleri vision
City-in-a-building. The choice
Is still ours to protect our
City of the future, our rumbling eggs
In our shatterproof test tubes—the perspective
Is of our choosing and we are
Victim by choice, our victory only that
We can choose. What are we
Doing here, Toby, Sandra
Hiding from what menace, sharing our
Microscopic nightmare, offering these cells
These souls, these bodies, to be a reasonable
Holy and living sacrifice to whom for what?

Strange what surrenderings we regret
The sorrow of our bodies given
Strange what victories we retain
The sweetness of our bodies given
Yet that June night of battle
Neither victory nor loss was felt.
An act as non-passionate
As taking a sleeping pill on a restless night
And briefly your shadow leapt through
The dark red channels of pre-birth
Exploded star bright into incandescent life
Palpitated in a cosmos alive with expectation.

For how many days did you
Grow wildly hopeful until your heart
Barely beating in an entirely new sky
Died. Black. My star child. I would
Wish for you another age, another mother.

Once did God
Flood away his imperfect creation
And now the imperfection remains
And an ark full of regret.
My small Noah, it is to another world
You must go, not the
Vacuum aspirator, fast-drying world
I walk on daily, not this
Morning and evening time heavy
Gasping to find laughter
Madness this dark mist stumbling.
I am Inuit mother pursued by starving
Beasts by night and howling blizzard
And I abandon you, here, here, in the
White numbing coldness, your face I dare not
Look at for an instant longer, you are
Dead before you are alive and I don't know how
My limbs move when it is I who
Should lie there with you, the foreign judge
Proclaiming my guilt and calling me
Murderer but my legs only frostbitten
Move on, stumbling in the perpetual winter

Farther away and farther always now to
Silences. I seek the silences how did
All this happen where did this
Come from this wild strange city
This long night of strange people
Strangers strangers strangers
Jungle creatures talking
Jungle talk jungle insects
Jungle beasts wild eyes there is
No escape only this secret scurrying
I understand henceforth every
Cockroach approach the

Scuttling disappearing I am
Familiar with the world of spray
With swatters what escape in this
Buzzing of flies in these
Patterns the air creates for them
Buzz buzz buzz buzz there is
Dance of web spider flea there is
This hole in which I crouch
Conspicuous in my craving for
A cloak of invisibility, imprisoned by
The eyes, the stars, within and without,
The constellations I reached and denied
With the denial by which I am denied

I am cut off I have
Trampled a universe I have
Transgressed the law of holiness
I have eaten the blood
It is my blood
Is it not my blood?
Those watery red tissues in glass bottle
Bits of debris, flotsam, fish skin
Is this my child drowning in a
Fiery sea this sudden tidal wave
This rush of mud over Pompeii
Can you hear the rushing child, this world
Is not for you, nor you not yet, for it
Nor I, we are dust, lint, speck, food for
Vacuum cleaners, we are blood together
In a maelstrom of Leviticus we are
Flushed out of caves in Moreau's island

Baby baby it is finished now
But stay with me stay in this
Perfect world let me keep you

Alive let me hold your warm
Body let me baby keep you
From the arguments this time, the schools, the
Newspapers it's a friendly woods we
Walk in on grass as soft as quilts
We are together in this deep soft trap
This well, this long falling I
Tripped the latch with my own hand
I have not stumbled I have rushed
Headlong towards the breakers
Carrying you tossing you from cliffs
I have burnt you on many altars
Offered you to the village elders
For their evening meals, my ram-child,
My Isaac without a saving God—

It is my faith that died
Long before you were conceived
And my ice-covered legs move more
Slowly now it is the love law
We must yet obey and how have I loved you?

Euclid was it child of your spirit
Hovering round my moon-hollowed night
Is it your ears I have deafened
And your dead universe now
In which I pray. Euclid the books tell us
The place of your birth is uncertain.
I confess I could not have stood
Your craving for perfection
Where did you go so quickly were you so
Uninsistent on life you died so easily
Could you not have fought a little at the oven door
Performed a mere Daniel in a den
Could you not convince me or this

Italian doctor, my accomplice, your father,
My accomplice, could you not through
The long wrestling night of excuses and lies
Shout down the executioner with his
"Life must die that life might live"
Was it you, Euclid, arguing with the moon?
Do you weight me now?

The tides do not return the beaches
Fill with harpooned whales
Cupid as harpoon king grows weary
And sleeps amid poisoned spears
Jonah lies rotting in the store-room
Nineveh is lost. You were
A small fish struggling for three minutes
On the prongs of a well-aimed hook
Are you somewhere now Euclid?
Was your angel not yet assigned?
Did we throw you back?

We swam upstream and discovered
The river was an eddy in a larger stream
The choices were ripples in a waterfall
The ripples fell like Niagara
How many stars drowned today
How many possibilities have been denied

My dream daemon leaves my night watching
But the waiting will return to the silences
The rainbow was a promise of fire
But new signs follow the holocaust
There are patterns more hidden than our patterning
Deaths more lasting than our murdering
There are celebrations still in the surety of death
And more resurrections than I have known

Friday. July '71. Ottawa.
"Dear Euclid," the dead moon has announced
"I am indestructible.
I am star."

Jericho Road

1977

For Gordon and Deidre

Poems for My Enemies

Bast, the Cat Goddess

the spirit of the cat goddess
stalks my walk through the
halls of the British Museum
pouncing at my eyes
a sleek black icon
lower Egyptian deity

an inaudible yowl
thin and commanding as
a magnetic beam pierces
the glass case

it is for this, for this,
for this you are made, to
pulse, to spring, to move
in an unapologetic dream

the hairs on my body
rise like iron filings

POEMS FOR MY ENEMIES

The will to love you lurks
behind my hatred like the
ghost of Christmas-to-come
with its armful of funerals
and its pack full of guilt

Since God and Dickens declare
a mid-death reconciliation
I stretch my elongated fingers
thinly in a silent
watching night—the wind
seeks edges and loses itself
in the vacuum

It is here I know as I wait
that angels will come rushing
in like fools

OFFICE POLITICS

the method is so minute
even the microscope of sleep
fails to outline its form

a whisper carefully placed
                              here
in this well-liked ear a
subtle questioning
a faint odour like leaking gas
a fury of speculation behind
doors between two friends or
three perhaps a trusted fourth
the creation of fact from fantasy
a gradual growth of conviction

the enemy is defined
by its absence, the threat
of its innocence demands
that guilt be verified
suspicion leaps to certainty
the monster gropes
onto the waiting stage
its tiny bullet eyes
ricochet around the room
seeking its creator

DIRECTIONS

"Come to me" he said
I couldn't believe it
he was intoning this
like ze grande pussycat
moustachio macho man
or oily latin-chanting
snake in the tree
trying to mesmerize
cheeping maiden bird

"I am gentle" he said
he was medieval then
suddenly—saints ablaze—it was
Jeanne d' Arc at the stake
all in flames and his
hands quick as brush fire
licking the white ribbon-tight
story of O dress that my
conscious sisters have
assigned to ridicule

"It's a mummy's
bandage you're waving—
some old death surrender signal"
they said "come to life" they
said "it's the twentieth century"

We were walking through the
British Museum surrounded by
old gods, old goddesses,
draped, naked, a
sarcophagus turned bathtub

fragments of columns
of yesterday and yesterday—
"this way" they said
clopping their clogs with confidence
on the marble floor

My timid sisters with
crepe-soled shoes squealed
and chirped
an army of sparrows
hopping down the hall

SHE IS WANTED

time unwinds his limbs
his sarcophagus bindings
his catatonic eyes readjust
he rises stiff as death

he steps into his van
"to serve and to protect"
he cruises the alleys
with searchlight and siren
and his many unknown weapons

she is wanted
dead or alive

blood drops on the rock pile
slowly sucking the stone
the red juice grows grey and granular

he asks her to sign
on the dotted line
beside the official seal
red and jagged as a saw blade

Therapist

he walks into the sphere with
his invisible mile-long shield
flattening people into
one-dimensional slabs on which
he draws his graphs and charts
carefully avoiding the use of
any four-letter words

he is Charles Atlas holding up
a flat-circle world and
talking to his audience in
balloon-enclosed messages

we are serious as children
with comic books we
believe in superman

DREAM OF KING MIDAS ASLEEP

we are small thieves in the woods
with our stolen gold
afraid we will be caught
and frantic for hiding places
in the basement of the castle
with our thousand tools
we are digging

upstairs the owner sleeps
rapidly I change my clothes
and approach his room
seduction is my salvation

in the grate by his dying fire
an envelope addressed to the world
curls into smoke a wooden signpost
unburnt stands in the ashes
the word on the sign is "Nameless"

I approach the stranger
his hands are covered in cotton gloves
earth and grass are in his grasp
as I recognize him, an alarm clock
chimes and hammers
"happy birthday to you
happy birthday to you"

BREAD TO STONE

turned to stone
she asked for bread
we offered cakes
and as she waited
the food
within her grasp
turned to stone
she asked for bread

LARYNGITIS

we form the first
microbes with our minds
the earliest anxieties
rattle through our bodies
visible sewage utterances
mucus, Tampax, turds,
we clog the system unwittingly
the backwater rises in the streets
we slosh through the stench
with hoarse bubbly cries a
drowning cat's underwater mewing
we swim like tiny Alices
in the pool of our tears
our throats corrode we
regurgitate phlegm, spit
tiny pointed arrows we are
struck dumb like John the
Baptist's father, the
plumber arrives with
emergency supplies his
plunger pumps our wordless
sins to the surface of our
dreams we are clutched
in spasms of coughing

Like Spearing a Butterfly

like spearing a butterfly
me in my dream
dead with a sword in my belly
the villagers scattering

night falls in
drops of flesh from a
rotting sun

a million hair-thin
spider legs leap from her skull
skeletal as wind
she approaches

without a word
she watches
her eyes grow fat

NIGHTMARE

for you, nightmother
these murderings
this offering of
bloodied infants
for your feasting

I have murdered
the world for you
why are you still so thin

if I strike you
blackness shall rush
from your devouring eyes

you cannot see
my innocent blood
on the blade

WASHDAY

how can the wash get clean
if the water is not clear
if there are buckets of mud
in the washing machine

it is true, after a while
the mud becomes very clean
after a while the scream
thins into silence, the corpse
turns to air after a while

already straw bodies
are wind-frayed
the heart pumps
clots of air
spasms of mud

time will change all this
the sheets will blow in the sunny weather
someone else will fold them

Footprints

and your legs must move
pumping blood through the brain
so your eyes can see the fire
in the darkness so your legs
can move in the right direction
if that makes any sense
and you keep moving but you can't
see the pillar of fire
or the cloud by day
you may be moving in circles you
don't know there is no
clear direction all you know
is that your legs must move
and your blood is on fire
and the eyes in the back of your skull
are tracing the footprints behind you

OR POOR CO-ORDINATION

since I was told that
every time you step on a bug
part of your foot bone crumbles
I endure this late-night house fly
pumping over my skin
with cold stickle tongue
its furry legs rubbing
its swivel-pin head

insomnia is a parade of pests
a thin-veined post-midnight
buzz in the room jolts me awake

its creaturely concern
keeps me sleepless

OVERNIGHT GUEST

It was only after the toilet flushed
I realized how he had glided
Silently past my open bedroom door.
During breakfast he found difficulty
Eating my heavy porridge words
And I saw his hand several times
Move to trip the lever and heard
The noisy gurgling of undigested thoughts
As they dropped below the trap door
Into an underworld of miscellaneous coughs.

FAUCET SOUNDS

night, and the dripping faucet
drums its own rhythm
he dams the reaching droplets
takes space, silence, withdraws
from the tap tap on his door.
morning, and he wonders
about rusty pipes and
plumbers' bills and they
look at pictures of new houses
with completely dripless faucets
"Next time I'm marrying a
sump pump" she says and
he talks of moving to the Netherlands

PHYLLIS WEBB ON THE CBC

I am sitting
watching the wall and listening
to you here in my kitchen
on the radio whispering
and the sound of your whispering
is food transformed to blood
sinew bone teeth person
thought and still somehow
I am sitting and watching
the wall

JOSEPH AND SALEENA

Saleena our formerly slinky cat
is pregnant as a potato sack
and sleeps at my feet on the bed
her bulging and lively lumps
leaping in her abdomen

every batch she births is
a multicoloured mosaic she's
fully Canadian, fat and placid
with wilderness memories

elsewhere the Joseph cat
with the multicoloured coat
is abandoned in the alley while
the grey coat white coat business
as usual brother hurries home
leaving Joseph in the night
dreaming dreams

THE AQUARIUM HAS ITS OWN SILENCES

feeling your letter this morning
while staring in the aquarium
colourful male guppies and
fat grey mother with babies which
cling to the camouflage of greens

and remembering that chunky woman of my childhood
her short bow legs and sturdy walk
her endless procession of children
and her handsome quiet husband
committing adultery with his secretary
the village rocking with gossip
when their baby bulged the secretary's dress

and the chunky woman left her brood one day
kerchief on, churning her legs, seeking
the edge of the village with her darting eyes.
I stared and stared the way
I stare this morning at these fish

your words dart among the pebbles
in the confines of my mind. I close
my eyes for love of newborn guppies
and flounder silently, the village
heavy in my veins

SPHINX

blood appeared on the dark sphinx brow
coursed its way down
to the ground

an hour obtains for us
several illusions

sunset
the earth has bled onto the horizon

sand dunes creep closer

BREAD FOR SALE

there's this no-good typewriter
on this ridiculously high narrow plant stand
in front of the store on a slanted hill
and no matter how you try
flicking the ribbon lever from white to black
to red and pound and backspace
the word *understand* won't come through
there's this typewriter sliding off
the plant stand and all the messed-up
papers mushing up the gears
and the invisible word punched on
and the whole heave-ho dropping
like dung down a huge hole
full of starving people—
and all the time the man in the store
lines his shelves with fresh bread

OFFICE TOADS

fat, hop-heavy
and bulbous-eyed
we watch for one
suspect step
our limbs leap-ready
risk no closeness

one kiss my swift
amphibious prince your
lasso lips your
glue-tipped tongue

toads, yes
but not for kissing

Snake Dance

a semantic dance, the
politeness pulses along
scales slippery with speech

from the slow long
dwarf star centre
gravitational pull of
submerged need the
body's coils recoil on
the skin of our lies

we smile the theatrical
smiles that mask our
moving, our minds are
almost mesmerized
into belief

The Success Ladder

with each rung we
ascend deeper into
our bowels we become
tortuous as intestines

we cling with our
signatures and our
cunning friendliness
we climb on the
labour of others

at the grinning end
at the slippery top
waits the hungry
serpent we worship

it spreads a table
before us in the
presence of our
enemies it
feasts on us forever
its cup overflows

GOLDEN CALF

and then there is this
great catastrophic animal
mechanized beyond belief
piston precision legs
bronzed to perfection
chugging like a train as it
marches down the laneway
every morning precisely at eight
to board the morning bus

the golden calf baby with her
clanky flanks moos among us
it is not a golden steer
but the hope of motherhood here
her unformed teats promise us
milk someday, justice someday
swimming pools, fun in the sun

like speed like heroin like
power like greed she wears a
thousand masks saying she is
Martha saying she is Mary
doing the better and the
necessary deed

soft as sleep she brands us
with the mark of the beast
when in our dream-webbed flight
we are caught in the fascination
of her light

with her strong metallic tail

she sweeps away our eyes
which hover like a swarm
of hungry flies

DAY ONE AT THE PMO

initially one is aware
of the odour of fur
of the hints of flesh
on the bared incisors

one notes the carefully arranged
surgeon's tools
on this reverse
island of Dr. Moreau

a chair with arms
a chair without arms
a carpet
a door
a window, two windows
a phone with buttons
a phone without buttons

initially one is aware
of scufflings in the corridors
one views the new
appearance of one's limbs
with alarm
initially

In the Almost Evening

In the almost evening loneliest time of day
I looked out the window and could see sky
and I said "Sky, what can you give me?"
and sky said "I can give you sunset." So I
looked at sunset with moon and star
and said "Sunset, what can you give me?"
and sunset said "We can give you skyline."
And I looked at skyline with bright lights
and I said "What can you give me?" and
skyline said "We'll give you people" and
I said to people, "People, give me love."
And people said "Too busy."
So in the almost evening loneliest time of day
I took to listening feverishly.

Old Man in the Library

old now and
nameless for me this
man in the library

like a beheaded flower
he blooms here briefly
in my mind's bowl
his stem, leaves, roots
elsewhere, in a room perhaps
nearby

fingers of both hands
cut to the knuckles
he adjusts his glasses.
smooths the newspaper,
opens and closes his mouth
making short clucking sounds

patiently, slowly he
tries several times to
turn the page

Raphael's "The Miraculous Draught of Fishes"

In London's Victoria and Albert Museum
Christ sits miraculously with two
Full-grown men in a
Boat tinier than a bathtub

His white robe
Reflects in the water
Red as a sunset
Red as a pool of blood

The sign says "The robe was
painted in a mixture of white
and a fugitive pink lake pigment
out of which the latter
has faded. In the reflection
the robe was painted in vermilion
a permanent red pigment"

A trinity of black birds
Flamingo-like creatures
Tread the water's edge

LEAVING HER WAVING AT THE AIRPORT

I am reminded of the three
red frozen apples on her
leafless December tree
which she said would gradually
disintegrate or disappear

small and wrinkled and
hanging in there till perhaps
the next snowstorm

DEAF PENSIONER

he terrifies himself
into submission
makes their decisions his
turns mouse-like
a garbage-can man
collecting orders
and mouse at the bottom
dreaming of dancing
always the dreams corroding
the base of the garbage can
dreams dancing the anvil chorus
in their frenzy to escape
while the orders gnaw steadily
along the edges
of his broken eardrums

HITCHHIKER

cars streaking past
and he says there are trees as well as cars
pain and benediction, parting
and meeting again
and that to believe otherwise
is to be a worshipper of cars
is to be a small animal sacrifice
on a busy highway

TULIP CENTREPIECE

in the restaurant
a small gang of
pre-teen girls with
cigarettes and makeup
clumped together as if
they'd been planted
in the middle of a
highway and ordered to
grow and each one
tough and surviving
like the pink plastic
tulip centrepiece they're
using for an ashtray

Rorschach

a startling garden
between austere green hills
some gigantic leaves on
long stems reaching for sun glory
and several overwhelming suns
odd varieties of rain
letters (initials?) on a potted cactus
and a chuff of wind
chasing petals across a desert

Stutterer

he kept stumbling off the polished world
silent with sandy tongue
at introductions
all his witty missiles
internally doused
"All children's veins should be cut at birth
because those who survive
will be stronger for having undergone the test"
she said slithering away
her tongue slicing the air
while he stammered

CONVERSATION IN MID-FLIGHT

from the air the prairie
is an inlaid floor a
giant landing strip
but within minutes we are
over the Rockies they are
still going strong

"... because I am not"
she says, "a victim because
I am not a victim"
her head is tilted slightly
back, her voice indestructible

his discomfort like a harelip
makes a reply difficult
he sputters like a defective
engine, there is nowhere to land

S FOR VALENTINE

"V for Valentine's Day" teacher said
Bobby drew black snakes on paper doilies
sharp S shapes from fat fingers
that curled inwards a
tight fist suppressing sounds
V for a white snake's belly
an angular snake propped open
V for open-heart surgery
he took scissors and cut
a jagged paper doily snake
shred it into snow specks instead

love could have been a burning flame
if she had told him
simply
that would have been enough
but there had to be ashes
grey hints in the daylight
of a bright dark night before
and in their cold cinder house
she flits about like the last firefly alive
trying to spark tiny specks of pain
with the soggy remains
of a previous evening's campfire.
he feeds her silence with an empty smile
asking forgiveness
for being unable to forgive
the fact that she has never once dared
to ask his forgiveness
simply

HOLUALOA, ONE NIGHT

lava, once liquid fingers
now stone rootlets on
Hawaiian beaches mixed
black with bleached coral and
stringy green growing things

holualoa, one night and you
naked as the centre of a
candle flame my hand burning
when in the suddenness of windows
your flesh turned magically to wind

we fled the first ray of daylight
streaking a dry path through the
fiery sea, the wind
marking the transition

the houseplants slept on the window ledge
the curtains flapped in and out
making no advance on the sky

blood once down the island
and waves, coral, tottering stones
our skin now a green webbed
lace of memories

ERASURE

the night I sleep in his house
I have a nightmare about a
tiny blue eraser baby boy I
want desperately to save but
finally I am weeping and
asking if after all it is
maybe ethically and morally
right to abort

I waken and hear him
sleeping nearby. How much,
I wonder, do we choose to die?
I rub the dreaming from the day
cover the mind's embers
with waking

To Scuttle the Moon

wandering, August evening, down the mall
to the lights spawning in the canal
a thousand low-flung baby moons
and fisherfolk groggy with bait
looking with lunar hooks
for late-night sea creatures

comes this man offering
candy, tidbits, a fishy stare
then—great endemic whale day—
he slops into my lap, a
tidal wave of blubbering—
is this a fisherman's reward?

I flounder from the taffy pull
to scuttle the moon and the sailing swans

like a witch and warlock busily gathering
ingredients for our separate brews
we kissed with fiendish carefulness
(with tenderness? try tenderness)
we were lacquered liars webbing love
the words in our lungs growing wings
beating at paper clouds (try
silence, try mystery) but the tightest
web like our honest cries defied the
struggle of our lies (try anything)

As Those Who Are Too Old

he is inventing me
but I cannot say to him
she is not real
even as he held me
he was destroying me
and creating her
he was puzzled when
I walked away
as fast as those
who are too old to die
he writes her letters
which I intercept
and answer with great care
and imprecision

Once When We Were Rejected

once when we were rejected by each other
(not fully rejected, not fully accepted)
he said "We're totally different people
what you need is a medieval knight"
and he was a modern forward man
scorning my reluctance to engage
and called me untimely

I was thinking of my once upon a time
when the world was flat, truly flat
disappearance defined the edges of our circles

and now it's spherical with full
returnings to our departures but soon
it will be neither flat nor spherical
but secret

and the secret world has many priorities
walking on grass, wading through oceans
sitting in the shelter of small protective shacks
but when I tried to sketch my secret map
he took his raft and disappeared
off the rim of a world

FOR PETER W.

you stand at the crossroads
your arms outstretched
directing traffic, maintaining
order, letting the
multitude go by to weep
or gambol or spit on the corpse

St. Peter of the traffic squad
in the middle of the throng
our shadows graze your face
as we rush by the small
candlelit signpost of
your open arms

ENCOUNTER

they met and sparked with the
speed of knitting needles each
click clack stitch picked
up without a hitch

beginning in separate sweaters
they unravelled as eagerly
as children at a seaside summer
flopped spread-eagle onto the
growing woollen blanket of
their easy intimacy

and swimming and scissoring
in the skein of their trampoline
they were two tangled kittens
with spring-tipped claws
momentarily hidden in a
woolly wilderness

WHEN THE ALIVE PACKED HIS SUITCASE

when the Alive packed up
and walked out of the day
he said he would write maybe
he said he might call

she had been the miller's daughter
refining the world, eliminating chaff
roughage and vitamins calling them
insensitivities, gross impositions she
used to say especially early in the
morning especially late at night

also she was the little red hen
planting wheat, harvesting grain
"Who," she would hoot, with feathered
first raised high, "will help?"

"Not I," said Alive, and on the
day she spread the bread with fresh
gooseberry jam, on the day she
ate him whole, he sat subdued and
refined as death, he left with no
forwarding address

It Wouldn't Be So Bad

if I were a brown cow on the prairie
by a water hole, lying on
thistles under the sun
never having lain on a double
mattress in an air-conditioned
apartment—if I were, I say,
a brown cow, placidly swishing
flies off my rump—

and if you were a crow
on a telephone post
having chosen of all the
miles of posts that
particular one without
days of indecision—

and you were to flap away
when the truck came roaring
down the highway

Being Limbless

this matter of having no arms and legs—
you feel it isn't fair and besides which
the whining offends sensitive ears
and so you sit there on the corner
with your long sleeves and long pants
dragging on the sidewalk
while the ladies and gents
prance past and stuff pennies
in your mumbling mouth
and so what and so what
it's just a matter of having no
arms and no legs and anyway
you end up saying who wants
to be a centipede

ABOUT HIS NOT BEING EXPLICIT

when he touches me
he does it with glances
he does not thrust his tongue
between my teeth
for he is tired of the taste of blood
he takes one look, no more
and covers me with flesh
when I ask in puzzlement
"What is it?" he says only
he has made me hear
what he wanted to say
without his having said
any words. when he leaves
I am convinced
he was never there at all
he runs in the wind
showering invisible glances
in his festival of flight

BIRD AND FLOWERING TREE

hummingbird humming in
nectar, in petals in the
shade of an overwhelming
flowering tree and saying—oh
insane bird with wings beating
the air—saying the sky is a
cloudburst of flowering

Fire Alarm

there are many ways to
care for fires, stoke coals,
turn dials, smoulder
under blankets and
damp leaves

by not calling for a week
you hope to ignite a blaze
you wait eagerly for the
wailing fire engine

it is that the meat
is always too rare
the flesh never quite
done enough

Sliver in Her Day

up out of the floor a slow
sliver in her foot she feels him
telling her to take her hands
her hands she touches the day
with hesitant glances moves
from the spot with a twisted
smile and limps, her hands
useless wings unwilling
to doctor her feet

As Though It Were the Earth

as though it were the earth
and the words were hoes, shovels,
garden tools stacked at
Eden's gates—I will
talk about love—
spade the earth bury my face
in the soil search for you everywhere
since each time we begin to meet
the angel stands flaming sword in hand

since words have dripped
open from the fruit's wound
and been planted in our limbs
and each wounding brings
a fresh outpouring

until the swords are withdrawn
or we wrench them free
until the words cease
until the wounding ends

SNOWDRIFT

how the sun defines it
the snow blowing up
thin as a shadow
tiny rockets of glare dust
forming a sharp drift bank
the wind carving a knife of sun drops

behind our half-closed eyes
the moon turns slowly
gathering the shape

The Wedlocked

On the Jericho Road

Your tongue
was your weapon
I lay silent
on the Jericho Road

Silence is also
a two-edged sword

These words
are my donkey

The Wedlocked

I
they did their measured
step down the aisle
forsaking all others—

with endless ring
"till death do us part"
till ashes to ashes

they seeded their bed
with promise and prayer
the priest and kneeling congregation
covered them with earth

2

they seemed compatible
Jack and Mrs. Sprat
one lean one fat
one laughed one wept
one gave one kept
one was early
the other late
one hated to need
one needed to hate

3

in summer she was
a fluffy woman
in her frilly bikini
flubbing across the beach
like an athletic chiffon cake

But in winter she became
iceberg woman
he turned his flashlight on her
—assault and battery—
imagining he was the sun

4

a bird in the hand is
better than two in the
blue-eyed bush better
than three in the open
fingers of a tree better
than all the birds in the
palm of the sky he said
his fist tight as a prize fighter's

5
he did the pinch test
his hands demanding the
not too soft
not too hard

when you squeeze, she said
the bruises spread
dark and red

6
eventually they ventured
to the marriage counsellor
like that fabled
couple in the dark
huddling around the stove
warming their hands
over the glowing coals
of a cat's shining eyes

7
they sought precision
they asked what really
was wrong
reasons flickered like
short-wick candles
they sat in the belly of
the night wind arguing
scoring points balance sheets
as if it were they
who could swallow the night

8
they agreed to be
from distances of sky dream

trapped forelegs locked
in their clinging need
day upon day they
agreed to stay through
slow death by soul rot,
routine, repetition, they
chose their familiar
wage-weary faces the
hard and dreamless
durable stone

the day's unkind truths were
splints and spears on their
fractured limbs they
cracked when they bent

with porcelain smiles with
carved conversations they
administered their marriage they
executed their lives

9
she sealed all doors
to keep the sand off the rugs
to keep traffic out of the house
she threw away the keys she
progressed through many silences
she identified with mannequins
surrounded by cardboard daisies
she stood all day in the mirrored room
the white chalk wound of her mouth
whispering "let me in
          let me out"

10

he grew desperate for more mirrors
framed or frameless, all shapes,
broken, chipped, distorted, he
suspended them from ceilings
lined them side by side
until the last window was covered

they were last seen as
flickering TV images, two glass bits
on the floor, lost in the will
of infinite walls

11

neighbours discovered them
clutched in plastic
a promise of flesh
capsuled before its birth
silence like a great ocean
had swallowed their edges

a calcified couple
wrapped in endless shawls
they carried a stale conception
and memories of war

ON THE HOME FRONT

off the shampoo bottle as well
not just off the toothpaste
he forgets the cap which I
take and plaster on the
white wall collage, a white
spot on my white spot
invisible protrusion on
invisible barricade the
house is booby-trapped a
microscopic militia guns us
down from behind the peelings
on the kitchen counter, from
the bathroom floor

TONIGHT NOTICE

a butterfly
emerging from its cocoon
voluntarily without prodding
the upside-down brown sky
branch of its emerging
dropping away as wings
walk the air

yesterday the bullet questions

tonight, notice
the armoured butterfly
plowing the brown sky

Post Mortem

early in the still grey morning
the left side of his face
wrinkled against the pillow—
on his forehead
just beneath the surface of his skin
a barely discernible ripple, a tiny mound
slowly emerging, waving tentatively
back and forth across the forehead
a worm, hesitantly
down the nose, into the left nostril
and out, moist and slithering
pulsing across the cheek, past the ear,
the hair, the pillow, down the sheets
onto the floor—
the knees buckle as the worm jerks
and out through the forehead
crawl intestines, kidneys, liver, bile,
and body shading to a powdery white
the skin wrinkling as the flesh recedes
and the room fills with a coiling
recoiling ooze—a final shudder and his
hollowed bones prance and prattle
clattering and grumbling as he
stumbles blindly to the bathroom

FIGHT # APPROX.?

he's gone curling, he has—
took himself down to
where they are, to the
slab of ice where there
are stones and brooms
and dead centres—and left me
here alone with two
sleeping kids and the
warning to be faithful
and lonely as hell—
he could've drawn circles
on me and swept brooms
across my icy brain, slid
stones to a focal point—
here I'm an empty rink
full of circles and arrows
he's telling me to be faithful

The Signs Were Everywhere

she was a fast-dancing
laughing leaping willow lady
an evening's delight—the signs
were everywhere and they were
eager then to go half-naked
and half-crazed into the night

now their touch is parched
as prairie, the sandstorms
blow over sun-baked skin
they did not know that moon
creatures sleep at noon and
lunar signs reverse their shadows
through every revolution of light

And You Talk and Talk

Walking barefoot through spring forest
mud, tanglebrush and mottled leaf
feet plastered with messages and
being barefoot in a warm forest
love words are compulsory
predictable as a TV serial

it is as if we have stepped
into an icy stream, the winter water
searing the clinging brown and revealing
a red cut trickling across our
leather boots

When He Was Conceived

when he was conceived
she was stone being carved
she opened to chisel
and the bit of crying
that hid in the rockiness
made the hard stone melt

when we were conceived
there were stones being carved
we asked questions
and from the valley came
the long long mist

Sampson

where the lights I see and
the lights I cannot see are
intricately woven round the pillar
where anger is a kiss

I swallow your thoughts
in my wish to love you

the lightning round the pillar
swallows the shadow
I am a shadow of a pillar
I hold the column
wondering if I have the strength

WANTED TO TELL YOU

wanted to tell you
I was sorry
but from the upturned
white fish belly
ugliness glowed
an ice-scabbed sun
wanted even there
to impress you
with a kindness I
did not feel

drift words
waves against a
northern glacier
and no birds watching
no moon no eyes
coloured lights
in a sky I'm told
I've never seen

waves rush
pity dash away
a shore of ice
grind hard oh sun
melt down rain
upon us

FEAR

I fear you
as I fear the
flower in the flood
drowned in the
river of rain

as I fear the
water-skiing fly
leaping from
flower to flower

and the fish pursuing
and the man
with his fishing net

FORTY BELOW

no fresh snow
no sleigh tracks, no angel wings
but ice crust
bulldozer scars
winter hides many secrets
its mirror has a hard surface too
the faces do not smile when we do
if beneath our waiting
the sun beams, the candle glows
we'll shine, burn warmly,
reach
melt

the way this flower grew
was not to my liking
I poked it impatiently
nipped it, drowned it out,
left it withering for years
thinking perhaps some miraculous bloom
would suddenly burst out
or hoping it might disappear
decay or dry and blow away
but it survived secretly
in its dusty hours
did not die
nor grow nor open
an amazing endurance
and patience which neither
blooms nor fades love is
patient they say

WILD ROSE BUSH

in the middle of our constant
penultimate argument he
went to the wild thorn bush
in the tame garden to
pick the rose, tugging and twisting but
finally, leaving it there he returned
and sat beside me, coughing softly while
the bent branch of the injured bush
moved with imperceptible grace
in the elastic afternoon

LEAF

this which once clung
on tree branch
which with cold and colder
wind was flung

this our leaving
rain trapped and brown
as earth and dung
soils our walk

with rake and plastic
garbage bag with
new coat and haircut
we bury the fall

Yet There Was Bathsheba

thinking about this holy matrimony thing
and old King David taking sacred food
from the temple to give his starving men
like we love-starved, life-hungry
marriage-broken warriors seeking
sacred love in holy places—our
inner heart of hearts tearing the veils
of lovers, counsellors, psychiatrists, whores
or who have you—feasting gingerly
beneath the cherubim while outside
rage Philistine doubts and guilts reminding us
that King David another time when thirsty
threw away the dearly won water
his men brought him, making
no game of his thirst and daring
to risk no life for love—
(yet there was Bathsheba
and all David's guilt triumphant
couldn't keep wisdom from issuing forth
from that unholy bond)

WORM

in the dream I was
squeezing my eyeball
between my two forefingers
managing to evict
three tiny multicoloured
worm-like wriggles

before falling asleep
crumpled in thick towels
tiny unkind truths
swarmed between us

and all night long
engaged in explorations
through fur, nuzzle and underbelly
the conquerors established
tenancy in my eyes
fought eviction notices
threatened blindness

Blue Eels

bright blue beaded eels
the fierce survivors
in my aquarium dream
beyond neglect and drought
and frantic cold tap water
which killed the last
tropical guppy,
these two cold sea things
as if created from
desert and winter, reared and
lurched like terrible horses

two more in another bowl,
young and light brown
not yet blue or bright-beaded
tore at a frayed and bleeding sunfish

yesterday, the house a maze of writhing circuits
we were as obedient as iron filings
bristling to unseen currents
our cold blue torrent of words
aggressive as metal
bled the sun

Walk in Aquarium

after our heavy talk we walk
to the aquarium and see in one tank
soft blue velvet fish yellow
striped ones with foxy faces
succulent sea cucumbers—and
beside this display, a sample
of current harbour waters with
crabs, some starfish, flounders,
a coke can covered in brown slime

after heavy talks it is not
always easy to forgive, the
words cling, unresolved debris
rests in waiting pools—it is
not always easy to remember
there are other ways to speak,
deeper waters safer
than this harbour

Found Art

when the garbage collector goes on strike
it is time to negotiate with
farmers and art collectors

I scatter seeds on yesterday's refuse
and look for objects which I can
present as found art

your fear, my love, that I
will find someone else is
the mad planter's fear of the burrs
that cling to his heart

She Learned

he took her wild protests
for wild protests

bewilderment watched
through the forest

saw a naked hunter
burying his catch

which lay ravenous
in its grave

she learned
to protest less

Open Marriage

walking at night under the
intermittent street lights
our shadows fade and grow
back to front, short to long
weightless patches of grey
over the skittering snow

like Peter Pan we are
in search of our shadows and
constantly checking, these
difficult days

The Reject Wife

quietly by telephone and
weeping to her friends she
fashions her pain into knives
she carves flesh with
ravenous hands, the ventricles
tough and chewy on her
sharp teeth, the strange
deceptively sweet taste of
vengeance is on her lips

she flings her broken children
into the streets, she is delirious
with liberation, they groan
in her nightmares, her legs
cannot move, she is weighted
by crimes she cannot confess
her body ages, in the morning
she forgets everything except
that she must survive

when next she is born an
incantation attends her birth
I hold her with gnarled hands
to my wrinkled breast
my milk is blood

SHE SENDS OLD PHOTOGRAPHS

I take the pictures
but not with match and flame
with fingertips and bandages
digging with careful fingernails
I peel the crackling memories
from his skin

brown as antique blood
brown as old frost on
dirty windows, I wipe the
dark stains from his eyes
my lips are red with rust

DIVORCE LAWYER

he clutched his forehead
as if his brains would gush out
saying that if she wanted spiritual advice
she should go elsewhere
meanwhile he advised her
on her legal rights

Last Letter before Decree Nisi

We tell the facts many times
until we believe, until we
know that it is so
but as long as I am calling you
I do not know you did not hear.

This is the burial day
which is more somehow
like a memorial to a memorial
the law here pronouncing
facts like a benediction
over our entwined corpses
"ashes to ashes to ashes"
could we have finally come to this
under these chilly sharp lights
cutting into the courtroom like smiles
that crack open our clay faces
and through which we peer
wide-eyed and wondering.

I wish I could mail
letters to you
but words cannot seal
or open what our eyes
could not see. Only can words
follow our flight.
We tell the facts many times
until we believe, until we
know that it is so.

Tumbleweed

I walked in the weather
feeling nothing
not the wind, not the rain
not the touch of falling leaves
seeing nothing
not the rainbow, the
brown angular trees
hearing nothing
not your voice
your question
I tumbled
gathering the wind
in my restless nest

One Does Not Ask

leaving the shine and clank
of metal ship for the
vine-entangled raft and
drifting downstream back
to the long prowling night
of leopards, lynxes, reptiles
in the dark

when we set out on our
explorations bravely over the
black waters we intended no
wrecked ship creaking on the rocks

strange this unmapped land
the street lights spit and disappear
lightning cracks, stiffened cats
crouch in the bushes, children flee

we call and call the
wilderness peers through our
glowing eyes one does not
ask for terror one has not
sought this transformation

"WHEREFORE WHOSOEVER SHALL EAT THIS BREAD . . ."
1 COR. 11:27

living with these two halves of
two nuclear families in this
atomic holocaust, the teenage tyranny
a daily fallout of brimstone and
radiation over the bombed kitchen the
tidy people frantic as ants the
messy ones placid as squash after frost

daily, this private Guernica
bite by bite we devour our way
through debris leaving each other
deaf, blind, arthritic, brittle as
communion wafers

we no longer say grace before meals

BIRD POEM

when Deidre was so angry she
could only droop with it after
hitting the wall so hard she said
her hand was broken and I
could hardly remember that much
helplessness and rage

I am prepared for many forms
of farewell, but this? a
bandaged wing, a wild bird,
my fifteen-year-old high school girl

I wait without push or pull
through rage and flight and
unexpected landings
as did my mother with her
long-distance night praying
her cage of arms
a net and nest

The Way You Say Goodbye

as we stand in the doorway
the orchestra accelerating
and the conductor, we don't know why
trips over his baton
our eyes suddenly confused
ready to laugh but
there are no words except our names

the audience thinking he
tripped on purpose
and standing and applauding

the way you say goodbye

SITTING IN THE PLANE AT LAST

sitting in the plane at last
streamers of flesh flapping
in the wake of my flight
fast as a cockroach journey
light switch on scatter to the
edges death is the dropping
of heavy face and form in the
panic of escape

you chose you are
choosing the avenues of spring
you rush to the melting
arms of new love you
trample the entrails of winter
hungry as a waking
bear you leave

rushing away from your
flight your face dissolves
and re-forms with the
defiance of a hurricane

to be free I must
pass through the
hurricane's eye

Poem for Wednesday

the report comes by
voice or pen, by telephone, by
letter or lack of letter

the calendar flaps tick pat
tick pat on white walls
air vent whooshing a
steady metallic endless
november of nurses doctors
porcelain people frozen in
edgy groupings around his bed
his body taut as a bent bow
eyes leaping like arrows
across the battleground between
winter and hope with winter
winning the anaesthetist watching
the weakening pulse

beneath the ice the lake
is an endless wound festering with
prehistoric murk, he sits in a
garden of anchors resplendent with
small darting shrimp colourless
in the depths, wife, children,
friends, mother, praying in the
ice-locked ark their patterned
dreams weighting the ends of
his buried rainbow and swirling
like coloured eels in the
swarming dark

I remember we were tender we
were tentative as lightning lost
in the dance of northern skies, no
word spoken no touch no greeting
or farewell, suspended in
the mind's landscape, the
morning's sun broom sweeping away
our footprints in the melting drifts

is it enough that we once
luminous yellow and green after rain
met secret elm, secret willow, each
tree breeze-shaped, our leaves
riotous with light, the brief hour
edged with sparrows grey and flitting
the tree roots unsprung along the
banks our hands leaping up the
sky's stairs the vines of our minds
branching in pinpoint strands of
touch and spring fireflies is it
enough?

I sit in the night garden dark
auditorium with questing hands
in the attitude of trees,
asking

what strange trick was this, Lord
that you stood us a moment in Eden
cut off our hands and commanded us
to eat that you command us now to
walk in a sudden water garden
without feet what strange trick
is this?

listening here at the edge of
King Solomon's courtyard in the
cloud of accusing rain, my tongue
a knife in the smothering crowd I
do not know King Solomon's knowing I
hand over the short wick flickering
light of his life I hear him plead
his hands bound in white mitts
along the steel bars, his eyes full
of the sky and the traffic sounds
overhead the twin night suns
chrome bars moving down the
freeway down the hallway the
leaping shadows of small animals
of his arms of tree branches
flitting from this dream of flesh
the wind saying "such a long
time" his last words on the
telephone "till wednesday"

the leaves in the forest make
rain noises as they fall I feel the
dry rain brittle in my eyes falling
into my lungs, my lungs he cried
straining in his hospital bed
on this forest floor brown and
sandy as his hair I lie down
on dead grass the autumn moss
creeping over my limbs strapping
me down strange rules and intricate
twistings the soil is formed of
fallen leaves will this too be
a blanket can I love enough now to
watch him live or die without knowing
how or why can I sit in this forest

as one of a billion fallen leaves
will this telling now blow
fresh tolerance through a forest
grown sick with jealousy? there's

no key to the closed door our
hands clawing on the rising hull
will you bring him back will you
bring him back will you
let him into the ark will you
let me into the ark will you
flood my mind with clues to this
strange trick you're playing I
hear the music they are asking where
the lord of the dance has gone
the receptionist typing, orderlies
pushing things on wheels I hear
anonymous feet in the waiting room
the sound of many children crying I
must let this go now, it is your
rule, not mine, you have declared
that your surrounding is released
by my surrendering you have dangled
us upside down you made this toy
world and wound us up to shed tears
if I refuse to cry now refuse to
play in your wind-up world refuse
to laugh at the trick if I refuse
if I say no say no

but it's dark here wednesday
never comes my hands uprooted my
hands crumbling I'll put down this
pen as well I'll wait by this
empty no longer with me river this

white breeze in a soundless
forest without trees

you recede with the softness of
layers of gauze here where the
not yet shadow falls quiet
as the moon I watch you
fleeing the thick wave

this abandoning this abandonment
crawls with love

Woman in the Woods

1985

This book is for David

For David

Bird Song

Flung from our nests
in the late spring
and ordered to fly
or die we are
weaned to the air.

In this our flight
Lord in this long
fall the call
is clear—

to rise to sunlight
through springtime
storms and wars with
wings grown strong.

But here these wind-trimmed
unformed bones
and tiny beaks

that sing
inaudible songs.

Garden Poem

"Marigolds," he said
rooting her firmly
in his garden bed
"are sacrificial plants
for garden slugs."

She wiped the telling slime
from red-rimmed eyes
grew dragon leaves at dusk
turned dandelion.

And in every neat
suburban lawn
she nestled her tiny
umbrellas down.

Rain Day in Beacon Hill

From the woods weeping green
and the lone bird calling
to this new house in this new suburb
its walls dripping white paint from
a blue-veined sky overcome with slush—

Two blocks away in the future shopping cemetery
under a soap and salt-washed sun
brittle bulrushes stand sentinel
silent frogs dive in a drying slough
beaver frantically gnaws a tree
snapping turtle snaps in futility
mud puppy, microscopic water life
water spiders, skaters, snails
crawling twig things, tadpoles
disappear down the roadside drainage
as if they had never been.

STREET WALKING

Walking through the locked-up suburb—
every locked door, part of a tunnel wall
every locked door, a denial of a resting place
the coach suggests her calves are developing
the calluses on her feet are
excellent for treading coals.
He suggests she will be grateful
when she wins an endurance medal.
She tells him he can have the medals.
They are too heavy and
clank in the dark.

GIVE US THIS DAY

In the bottleneck places
people cluster
at the doorways of blazing buildings
at the bridges of bombed cities—

In this doctor's office
we have waited all day
for the filling of a welfare form.

Is it that we need more
doorways? More bridges?
More doctors? More work?

The answer lies at the heart of the flame
in the hour of suffocation
or the waiting game.

Shadrach's angel will find us
in the heart's fiery places.

WHERE THERE'S A WALL

Where there's a wall
there's a way through a
gate or door. There's even
a ladder perhaps and a
sentinel who sometimes sleeps.
There are secret passwords you
can overhear. There are methods
of torture for extracting clues
to maps of underground passages.
There are zeppelins, helicopters,
rockets, bombs, battering rams,
armies with trumpets whose
all at once blast shatters
the foundations.

Where there's a wall there are
words to whisper by loose bricks,
wailing prayers to utter, birds
to carry messages taped to their feet.
There are letters to be written—
poems even.

Faint as in a dream
is the voice that calls
from the belly
of the wall.

THE INSECTS IN OUR HOUSE

The insects in our house eat
holes in our clothes take
wood from our walls drink
water from our wells. The
insects in our house bite
dreams from our skulls in the
morning in the late-night tossing
the lace makers
the embroidery bugs the
invisible commuters scuttle
back and forth beneath the
floorboards in the
rafters along the arteries
in the bone marrow.

ANT AND BEE POEM

Love, I say, meaning
glue, as in I
glue you to
everything—the
sky, the kitchen
cupboard. I glue you
to this letter that
I seal with moist
tongue and Love,
I say, meaning
food, as in
send me your
round nubby words
to taste, the sweet
chewy texture of
honeycomb wax
and Love, I say,
meaning hunger and
this flung apart
longing and the busy
ants on the cupboard wall
carrying bits of sweet wax
home.

ETIQUETTE

The distance between her mouth and her plate
is the hesitance of her need
to devour each morsel of personality
she encounters at a feast. Oh etiquette
of napkins and spoons and upright pose
and soundless chewing, how eagerly
she would dispose of you and eat
with primitive zest.

ELITISM

is a cumin seed
you place between
your teeth—its
shell as intact
as unhusked wild rice.

Bite—
and the sudden
release of flavour
is a tiny assault
in your mouth.

The husk falls free
and departs
to its husk heaven.

Meanwhile
the rest of the meal
bows to cumin—

cumin bread
cumin salad
cumin curry

Here We Are a Point of Sanity

Here we are a point of sanity
while cars are leaping
over the edges of mountain cliffs
and someone broadcasts that the victims
will be lucky if they live
and there's a skyful of smoke from the wreck
and we're holding a hose and shooting water out
from way up here on top of a mountain.

For what? For what?

What we need are people on the scene—
healing people crazy people
people with seven league boots
and ready arms to
carry the rage. What we need
are shovels and axes and
mad mad friends
to plunge to the bottom
unafraid.

Oh leap down leap down
to the thirst
to the flame.

LAST DAY

That day, walking to work
the last day of the world
seeing everything for the last time—
the sidewalk café empty
a cabbie sleeping in his seat
office workers walking in the wind
everyone conspiring
to make the last day
as normal as every other.
The air swished up through the vent
making the calendar dance on the wall.
The riveters on the building next door
continued to break concrete.
The stenos clacked the typewriter keys.
The girls in the hall
talked about their babies.

That day walking to work
the sun low on the horizon
red and huge, an erratic sunset—
everyone decided not to notice
not to stare
and in the elevator
no one tried to be
unusually friendly.

The Devil's Spoor

Every previous unthinking
New Year's Eve,
a ritual murdering.

This year, you fear
the child may not
return unharmed.

Or if you refuse
to make this offering
death may rage.

This year, this time
you plead
you say no.

And suddenly
the mark on the floor—
the devil's spoor

white as dried
bird droppings—
thin communion wafers—

fragile
powdery food.

Ambivalence

Between two limbless lumps of hay
the donkey stands and starves.

With deliberate donkey dancing then,
choosing legs before choosing hay.

For David

Not as we dreamed or planned
did life fling us
nor by thought's search
did we find our way
but by walking
were limbs discovered
and the pathway formed.
Chance and change
not of our choosing
uncovered what was decided.

GREETING MY FATHER

I can hardly remember
the last time I wore heels—
clack clack clackity clack
on the marble floor
at the bus station—
assert assert assert—
yes, this is how it was
in the arrogant hair-bouncing days
before failure.

Father, I have come to greet you
wearing a mid-calf skirt.
Twelve guests will be coming
for a dinner in your honour
at my ex-husband's luxury apartment.

Isn't it almost
as you would have wished—

FORGIVENESS

The fruit takes of the sun.
The skin swells thin green
to red to ripeness
until the time for giving
when the wind
thuds and seeds the earth
and the rich brown soil
receives the flight down.

And to walk at that moment
in the orchard again
when the children
are still small
and to see
in the sunlight
how the blossoms are falling.

TRILLIUMS

Sudden in late
April forest floor,
white trilliums
bright epitaphs
brief memories of winter.

Last December
the sun no longer
melted the snow.
Snowflakes fell
in the glittering air.

With flattering words,
futile promises,
with such devices and
conspiracies of ice
the winds erected a tomb.

But from below
in Ontario, always
in springtime—
trilliums.

She Flees

PARTING SHOTS

He is sitting in a puddle
of hairs there, in a
forest of bulrushes and
swampland trees. He is
sitting watching the small
kingfisher bird and the twig
and the blue. He is watching
all the land around
morning moving slow as
sleep and snail. Even the
flight of birds is caught
on film. And still as a
cat's startled stare he sees
the falling bird its
one wing lifted forever
as it salutes the earth. And
here the rifle and waterproof boots
and there the camera and—
Click, the latch. Click
the tiny language of
terror. Don't
go please, he
says, without at least
breakfast.

He Is Not a Fence Sitter

He leaps over fences
as if they've been built
for no other purpose.

He will not, he says
stay stuck on a picket.
It's for the making of scarecrows
it's for people who flap.

Swift and decisive
in a featherless flight
he leaves like a bullet
and does not wave.

Black holes are formed
where he comes and goes
he's a wingless bird
a cosmic scarecrow.

TARANTULA

Dear Tarantula, strange friend
venomous with a longing to touch
and tyrannizing by the swift
sorrow of your stealthy sting.

What you want what you want
is to touch the faint
heart beneath the armour spread
division through its regular beat.

What you want is to ascend
the throne of your dissonant world
and feast on all the assymetrical
small and edible dyings.

She Has Fled

She (the wife
the nameless one)
has fled
to where the
name tree grows
its leaves
in the breezes
rustling.

And he
stripped bare
sits where she
sat before.

His arms
grown moist
as snail's eyes
search
the sky where
two small kites
are flying

seeking
strings.

Grief Poem

O that after all no
thought breaks
the mind's cold spell.

Chilled
these bones, their
language lost.

In this fresh silence
weather hides all
odours of decay.

By freezing time
I travel through
this numb day.

Look look
my small
my beautiful child

the icicle here
how it shimmers
in the blue sun.

My small
my beautiful child
look once more.

The Morning She Leaves

The morning she leaves
the sky is the colour
of the charcoal blue pigeons
that strut on the roof next door
and an endless double row
of curly branched winter trees
submit to the pruner's sheers.

The morning she leaves
the sky is thrashing
with dark pigeon wings
and dead branches
are gathered like hay.

AFTERWARDS

After he took
the budgie to the vet
and a needle pierced
its thin feathered belly
and it died
its arthritic claws clutching
nothing—

After he
cleaned the cage
and threw out the
leftover seeds and gravel
after he made the room
clean and neat—

what remained in his mind
was the budgie's grey claw
unnaturally straight
and his small daughter's
forefinger curved
stroking the tiny head.

It Dies by Detour

The honey bee slaps crazily
against the bus window
its intricate map-dancing
journey between nectar and hive
scrambled against the
transparent wall.

Zoo Scene

"Egyptian Vultures
Neophron Percnopterus from
Southern Europe, Africa and India."

The chicken-sized birds
have white and black tail feathers
yellow faces, black hooked beaks.

Taxidermist birds,
they eat two white rats
carefully through the anus
so neatly no fur is torn.

People squeal as they pass
"Lookit, they're eating rats
O lookit how they're eating."

One dark-skinned youth says
"'Ya gotta start somewhere,"
and his blonde girlfriend whispers
"Yay Egyptian."

EXPERIMENT

First a series of
tamed and tameable rodents
raised in cages with
mazes, food pellets, electric
shocks, gloved hands.

Next a wild rat
fresh from foraging through
wheat fields, rain storms
dodging predators with
brilliance
with wizardry
a warrior of the woodlands
a general bearing scars.

The researcher reports on
helplessness in animals.
He says the wild rat swam
for sixty hours
before it drowned.

He publishes his article
in Psychology Today
and makes an addition
to his curriculum vitae.

WIND POEM

When the window is open
and the night enters,
blinds flap
branches scratch the roof
the candle is blown out.

We pull the blanket higher.
Our hungry fingertips
pick berries in the moonlight

and there are no mosquitoes
or blackflies
because the wind is blowing.

If Your Mirror Breaks

If when you are holding a
hand mirror while sitting
in the front seat of a car
and the mirror breaks
you must stop everything quickly
step on the brakes
leap from the car.

If when you are holding in
your arms a mirror and you
feel the glass sudden in your veins—
if your throat bleeds with
brittle words and
you hear in the distance the
ambulance siren—

If your mirror breaks into
a tittering sound of tinkling glass
and you see the highway stretch
into a million staring splinters
you must stop everything gently
wait for seven long years
under a sky of whirling wheels

If your mirror breaks
oh if your mirror breaks—

JACKS

Seven geese in the sky
changing formation
the way jacks fall
five and two
four and three
your fingers scooping them
deftly off the tabletop.

CERTAIN ANTS

Certain ants
in seasons of rain
cluster together
into ant balls
that tumble over
troubled waters
till they touch
dry land.

In this season
of much drowning
much clutching
and clustering
it is enough
to breathe
occasionally.

In the Woods

AUTUMN

A wrinkled leaf
has fallen into
the cup of tea.

Instead of drinking
we ponder the shape.

MUTE MUSIC

No sound
but that breath
is round with speech
and all the trumpets
surrounding Jericho
sound the same note.

Mute music
undemanding
as the shape of doves
cautious and private
as the shedding of names.

Empty
is the city
in which even the hiding
is hidden.

FOR A BLANK BOOK

I have peculiar
leaf shaped ears.
My fur is
forest coloured.

When your flesh
first uttered words
I lost understanding.

You said I attend
stone and not flesh
source and not blood
bread and not bone—

your flesh
your blood
your bone—

which brings you to
mistrust of me.

And all the while
the stone bleeds
the source calls your name
the bread is broken,

but you cannot see
or hear
or taste.

Listen then, my love
to the wind blowing

and the sound of breath
over the grassy forest floor—

but know I did not bend
to the right or to the left
all the while
that I loved you.

DOWN BY THE WOODBINE

Down by the woodbine by
the woody glade along
the route of dragonflies
and dragons she
glides there where the
lily lie lily down
waters flow while
aloft the dragons
fly through the windy
wall of tall grasses.

She hears them there.
She fears them there
for sudden as a
swamp invaded by
speech—oh—

down they sway
and down again
their whispers swift as
frogs' tongues that
covet wings.

Deep in the woodlands
in the heart of the shadowy marshes
the black-gowned winged ones

with dark lanterns are
watching watching
their low chants
rapid murmurs
in a midnight crypt.

COALDALE POEM

In the heat of summer
Coaldale is full
of bluebottle flies
rasping at the windows—
small print gossipers
petitpoint buzzards.

Coaldale dear Coaldale
your dot and tittle preachers
your black-winged puritans
tell me how I may not live
or write of love.

Since what I've written
is forbidden I take
the small pink eraser
on the end of my pencil
the flesh of it
soft on my lip
flesh erasing flesh.

Gem of the West
I remember you
town of the fly swatter
town of the uncaressed.

THE RIDDLE OF NIGHT

The dryad faced three riddles—
the riddle of morning
the riddle of noon
and the riddle of love.

The answer to the
riddle of morning
was wonder. She was
tired of the definition
as the place to begin.

Dancing attended the
middle riddle but
the third was a
silent falling.

At night the dryad
fell into a stone well
to stars reflected in
the well's dark bottom.

Daybreak extinguished
her night-long flight
and the dryad wakened
to the riddle of light.

Moon Walk

Take care in the night travellings.
Walk into traffic with light feet.
The moon's highways are crowded,
the sky full of dust.

Walk gently in the night crossings.
Your side of the street has the shortcuts.
In the end you will come
to the spot where you first met.

The police are not watching
and jaywalking meets no disapproval
but walk carefully, the streets are wide
and traffic thick as on earth's freeways.

I have come on behalf
of the United Jewish Appeal
with the slogan "We Are One"
tattooed on my timid gentile heart,
wearing my "Why Not" button on my
blue winter parka, announcing
the East and other categories.

I am sitting at our
table of differences
declaring the slogan
to all who come.

Listen!
The sounds of fingernails
under the table
are sharp as the teeth of mice.

Forgive me.
I am obsessed with history
and always scratching for clues.

Train Trip

Sitting beside the strange
man on the train, she
hangs her coat over his,
the hood covering
his brown collar, the
blue arm bumping
bumping against the
brown elbow patch.

Intimate
the clothes caress
in the rock rock of the train
while discarded on the seat
they travel together
polite as death.

STRANGE GREEN SHOOT

Strange green shoot in this
middle-aged garden. Is it
weed? Is it vegetable? Do I
pull it out now or wait
to see what it might be.
I grow more curious
than executive.

Every minute its
roots descend through
skull through throat
leafing underground foliage.

Too late for uprooting
but here's scissor in hand
bleeding to dust
this thin green thing.

Mistress Wary and contrary
how does these days
the garden grow?

With dust and ash
with ash and dust
and fine white fragile bones.

ONE NIGHT'S STANDING

In all that seamless night
the one tearing
lightning rift
flashed blindness upon her.

Like the sun
breaking through a
black-gowned sky
for a moment
he shone into her
night-wide eyes.

Then without breeze or caress
in the time of the withered leaf
he disappeared

leaving her to journey
with one sense less
towards senselessness.

Dream

The boy child lies drowning
heavy and unfloatable as metal
his right foot hooked by
her foot. He is
lifted by the heel. He
is dangled upside down to
clear his lungs.

Achilles by the
heel comes healing.
By our weaknesses
we are hooked.

Note to a Gentleman

The time
to talk about your wife
is before.

It is the difference
between a shield
and a sword.

And if you want the battle
to be fought without arms
bring her with you.

Minerals from Stone

For many years
androgynous with truth
I moulded fact and fantasy
and where they met
made the crossroads home.

Here the house built
by lunatic limbs
fashioning what is not
into what might be—

a palace cave
for savage saints with
hunting knife still moist.

Bring me no longer
your spoils, my lioness,
I have a house in the
shadows now and have
learned to eat minerals
straight from stone.

ROAD BUILDING BY PICKAXE

The Highway

Driving down the
highway from Revelstoke—
the road built by
forced labour—all the
Nisei having no
choice et cetera et cetera
and mentioning this in
passing to this Englishman
who says when he
came to Canada from
England he wanted to
go to Vancouver too but
the quota for professors
was full so he was
forced to go to Toronto.

Found Poem

Uazusu Shoji
who was twice wounded
while fighting with the Princess Pats
in World War I
had purchased nineteen acres of land
under the Soldiers Settlement Act
and established a chicken farm.

His nineteen acres
a two-storey house
four chicken houses

an electric incubator
and 2,500 fowl
were sold for $1,492.59.

After certain deductions
for taxes and sundries were made
Mr. Shoji received a cheque
for $39.32.

The Day After

The day after Sato-sensei
received the Order of Canada
he told some of us Nisei
the honour he received
was our honour, our glory
our achievement.

And one Nisei remembered
the time Sensei went to Japan
met the emperor
and was given a rice cake
how Sensei brought it back to Vancouver
took the cake to a baker and
had it crushed into powder
so that each pupil might
receive a tiny bit.

And someone suggested
he take the Order of Canada medal
and grind it to bits
to share with us.

Momento

Trapped in
a clear plastic
hockey-puck
paperweight
is a black ink sketch
of a jaunty outhouse.

Slocan Reunion—
August 31, 1974
Toronto.

May 3, 1981

I'm watching the flapping
green ferry flag on the
way to Victoria—
the white dogwood flower
centred by a yellow dot.

A small yellow dot
in a B.C. ferry boat—

In the Vancouver Daily Province
a headline today reads
"Western Canada Hatred
Due to Racism."

Ah my British
British Columbia, my
first brief home.

For Issei in Nursing Homes

Beneath the waiting
in the garden in
late autumn—how
the fruit falls without
a thud, the white
hoary hair falls and
falls and strangers
tread the grey walkways
of the concrete garden.

How without vegetation how
without touch the old ones
lie in their slow days.

With pickaxe then
or dynamite

that in their last breaths, a
green leaf, yes, and
grandchild bringing gifts.

STATIONS OF ANGELS

Within the universe of flame
in the time between
watching and waiting
are the fire creatures
holy and unholy
hungry for those
many coloured parts of us
which have no names.

Blow out the candle, friends
quickly, and let us
close our eyes
while the devouring
is at hand.

At the heart of our stillness, in
peaceable flames we shall
hear
shall we not hear
our mothers
singing.

OLD WOMAN IN HOUSEKEEPING ROOM

Feeble star rays
leave the surface of her slow turning
hoping to find out there in the night
someone that needs
her needing light.
But stars die, she knows
eventually the spinning ends
lights sputter across uninhabited moons
and people who once were needed
no longer are.

Though she has extinguished
all the beacon candles in her dark
she still flickers—
a small flesh candle—
round and round
in her lighthouse.

JULY IN COALDALE

July in Coaldale and
so hot the scalp steams
and I am curling my mother's
fine white hair with her
new mist curler iron
I bought for her
81st birthday and
she is telling me
of her early morning dream
that it was Christmas and
there was music. "I can't
remember the song" she says
but after a few more curls
she is singing in Japanese
"Joy to the World"
somewhat out of tune
because she is deaf now
and her throat is dry but
she was famous for her
singing once and
she says in her dream
there was an old dry plant
that started to bloom.

CALLIGRAPHY

My eighty-one-year-old mother's
penultimate act
before leaving her house
of thirty-one years
was to kill
a large black spider
that sat still as death
on the bathtub ledge.

The calligraphy lies
a foreign word
of curved spider legs
delicate as brush strokes.

She Has Been Here for Three Months

She has been here for three months
silent as a saint on trial and
regal as a snow queen. Sometimes
with a sudden smiling grace, a
child's face, she moves through the
nursing home thick with
stammering woodpeckers in her
private popcorn tree country.

Gone from her familiar orchard
to a glacial whiteness she picks
with great delicacy the fruits
of her new winter trees.

Daily she waits for her
grandchild's letters—
sometimes on walker
sometimes in wheelchair.
She breathes the country odour
of last fall's hay
and watches the dandelions
growing white

and whiter and blowing finally
tiny umbrella puffs
across the open field.
And everywhere she sees
the earth bled to stubble—
dry as husks of hay
dry as egg shells.

It is time, dry time
all crying past.
It is time burning
burning in the air
and the small white
dandelion seedlings
are smoke trails showing
the pathway home.

I CARRY THIS FLASHLIGHT

I carry this empty flashlight to the store
along a street of dormant winter trees
to buy batteries
so that I may go to the basement
to replace the burnt-out fuses.

You are standing in the marketplace
in your hardware store
full of electrical fixtures.

The furnace in the basement
hasn't clicked on in hours.
I read last night
an old couple were found frozen
sitting in their kitchen.

I am carrying my flashlight
to your store.

In the Forest

In the forest the tree
perfectly balances its hours.
In the time of its branches
no branch is accidental.

In the forest our arms
perfectly balance the breeze.
In the time of our departures
no leaving is accidental.

In autumn
in the bare room
by a crack in the window
a curtain moves

as the woodsman arrives
precisely beyond time.

Through All His Days His Jokes

Through all his days his untimely jokes
were a stream of consciousness
constant spring thaw flooding into
any solemn or serious occasion.
Like summer in its exuberance uttering
flies, mosquitoes, zeppelin hornets
he would arrive with his harvest of cheer.
And here now at his autumn grave
the bird smiles, the grasshopper smiles
the tree sheds its leaves with
riotous shouting. All of earth
shares his mirth. "It's only
woolly winter I'm missing" he
says chuckling "These untimely things
happen to us all."

BOBBY GRAY—FEB. 20, 1981

We walk
through the brain's wide roads
seeking you
in the wintry sky.

You shine.
You smile.

Ah, and ever is
our dying thus—

One moment we attend
the brain's singing
then
we are the song.

Offerings

what you offer us—
a soap bubble
a glass thread—
what you place
in our open hands
one branch of
one snow fleck
a sliver of smoke

and if and if
the offering bursts
breaks melts
if the smoke
is swallowed in the night

we lift
the barricades
we take the edges
of our transience
we bury the ashes
of our absences
and sift
the silences

Fish Poem

Moving into the slow
pool beneath the voices
to the quiet garden where
airtime sounds are
cloud shadow and
sun games. What
matters here in this cool
inverted sky are small
darting fish
coloured cues shimmering
past the hooks, beneath
the nets, succulent, safe
and swift as prayer.

Dance Lesson

The dance master
dances in the tunnels,
in the bone marrow.
Crippled, he cries
that any awkward step
must do.

Here then and here are
these gentle deformed ones
holding the limbs
of the swaying sounds.

How beautifully music
moves in the air
with the dance master naming
our names like a song.

WATER SONG

who once on singing
water walked
on water still
walks he
in atmosphere
so dense in miracle
we here find fins
for diving
for flying

Selections from
A Garden of Anchors

2003

POLICEMAN AT YOKOZUKA

raining and as usual
lost and sleepy and not
knowing where to go
ask to rest and sleep
and when i wake i'm
covered by a blanket—
rice balls beside me
and a policeman with a
constant smile watches as i
wake and wipe the dry
spit off my cheek—we
talk and all the while
the sun steams the rain
to mist and all the
policemen in all the world
are as warm as the
green tea he pours for us
and finally when he asks
to see my passport i
know it is not to
mutilate

SMALL ROCK

they didn't know it was a small rock
in the middle of the road
cause the bike to swerve
and hit the ditch
what was real was his being
smashed open and ambulances wailing
and everyone weeping—
the little lie was never blamed

GREY LADY

within the new glass-walled office
the grey lady crept
with her scrub bucket and her mop
scouring the scars
the black heel skuff marks of the man
against the pockety pock dents
of the high heels
the scrub lady toiled
on hardened knees, leather-encased hands
her own soft moccasined feet
leaving no mark on the floor

WILBER TO THE DAWN

(for Wilber Sutherland 1924–1997)

and so, dear friend
still bound as we are here
by tides of human bonding
we have gathered to applaud
the journeying

and you
who, so far as I can tell
from heaven came
and to heaven have gone
and while on earth
made heaven home

from living room to living
room you go
while we in this garden
or that, as Mary sat
in various states of unbelief
wait for the great surprise

how happily you lived
without disguise
in all your every moment
book-filled speaking days
in boat or beach or tent
or auditorium, in church
and synagogue and meeting room
and deeply in the words and
ready arms, Wilber
with your eagerness to
serve

you did that
hour by faithful hour
and with such willingness of heart
in the service of your truths
and of the god we both call
love

within this universe, I pray
you still move, you live
and have your being in this same
element of love where we
this side of Eden
toil

until like you, to the tomb
we come, that
busiest place of the
holiest one
in the journey to death
that is wholly
undone

Wilber of the onward way
Wilber to the dawn
I celebrate with these
your many loves
a well-sung song
for you drank freely,
again, so far as i can tell
from the sweetest well

Acknowledgements

For family and friends too numerous to list, mostly in Toronto and Vancouver, for the long companionship of the Memoiristas, Kate Braid, Heidi Greco, Susan McCaslin, for Mary Lou Dickinson, Margaret Hollingsworth, Stuart Philpott, for JCSJ, (Japanese Canadians for Social Justice), for the Church of the Holy Trinity, for neighbours at the Toronto condo, for all who stood with me and Ann-Marie Metten of Kogawa House when the storms blew, for Judge Maryka Omatsu and Susanne Tabata, for my doctor Joseph Yu Kai Wong, for my prayer partner, David Walsh.

A thankful heart for Kelly Joseph's constant support. And for Canisia Lubrin.

In my January 2023 diary, on the day I met Canisia, I wrote in large letters — SO BLEST, SO BLEST, HOW CAN I BE SO BLEST. I feel I've known her beyond my life.

And for the person who saved my life but doesn't want to be mentioned.

Now in old age (eighty-eight) with this book, my last hurrah, thanks be.

This book is dedicated to the memory of my parents, Goichi Gordon, who showed me what forgiveness looks like, and Masui Lois, who exemplified truthfulness and dignity.

JOY KOGAWA is best known as the author of *Obasan* (1981), which is based on Joy and her family's forced relocation from Vancouver during the Second World War when she was six years old. Joy's other books for adults include *Itsuka* (1992, published as *Emily Kato* in 2005), *The Rain Ascends* (1995), and *Gently to Nagasaki* (2016). Her works for children are *Naomi's Road* (1986, 2005) and *Naomi's Tree* (2009). Since 1967, Joy has also published several poetry collections, including *A Choice of Dreams* (1974), *Jericho Road* (1977), and *A Garden of Anchors* (2003). Among her many honours, Joy has received an Order of Canada (1986), an Order of British Columbia (2006), and, from the Japanese Government, an Order of the Rising Sun (2010) for "her contribution to the understanding and preservation of Japanese Canadian history."